Pay us what you owe us...

REPARATION

The fight to bury the ghost of chattel slavery in the Caribbean

Mike Henry

LMH PUBLISHING LIMITED

First Edition
10 9 8 7 6 5 4 3 2 1

Cover Design: Roshane Mullings
Cover Illustration: Courtney Robinson
Photos: Jamaica Information Service (JIS)
Graveyardwalker (Amy Walker), CC BY-SA 4.0 <https://creativecommons.org/licenses/by-sa/4.0>, via Wikimedia Commons
Book Design, Layout & Typesetting: Roshane Mullings

Published by LMH Publishing Limited
Suite 10-11, Sagicor Industrial Park
7 Norman Road
Kingston C.S.O., Jamaica
Tel.: 876-938-0005; 876-938-0712
Fax: 876-759-8752
Email: lmhbookpublishing@cwjamaica.com
Website: www.lmhpublishing.com

Printed in the U.S.A. ISBN: 978-976-8245-86-1

CATALOGUING-IN-PUBLICATION DATA AVAILABLE AT THE NATIONAL LIBRARY OF JAMAICA

Pay us what you owe us...

The fight to bury the ghost of chattel slavery in the Caribbean

Another River To Cross

Mike Henry

LMH PUBLISHING LIMITED

Contents

Dedication

- **Dudley Thompson** *(Pg. 10)* • **Prof. Verene Shepherd** *(Pg. 26)*
- **Moses Nelson** *(Pg. 23)* • **Hon. Frank Phipps, OJ, QC** *(Pg. 48)*
- **Philmore Alvaranga** *(Pg. 23)* • **Sir Hilary Beckles** *(Pg. 66)*
- **Lord Anthony Gifford** *(Pg. 24)* • **Barry Chevannes** *(Pg. 89)*
- **Barbara Blake-Hanna** *(Pg. 26)*
- **Dr. The Hon. Ralph Gonsalves** *(Pg. 108)*

To name a few of those who have fought on the reparation battlefield

and National Hero **Marcus Mosiah Garvey**

and **'Jah Rastafari'** *who carried the*

battle for reparation and repatriation

Martyrs to the Cause of Reparation

Right Excellent
Paul Bogle

Right Excellent
George William Gordon

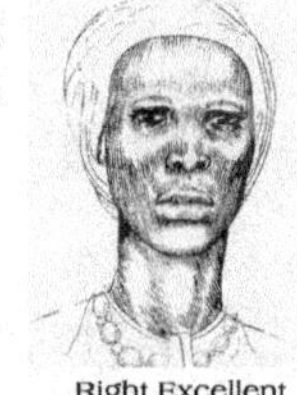

Right Excellent
Nanny of the Maroons

Right Excellent
Sam Sharpe

Cudjoe Lewis

Chief Tacky

Prologue

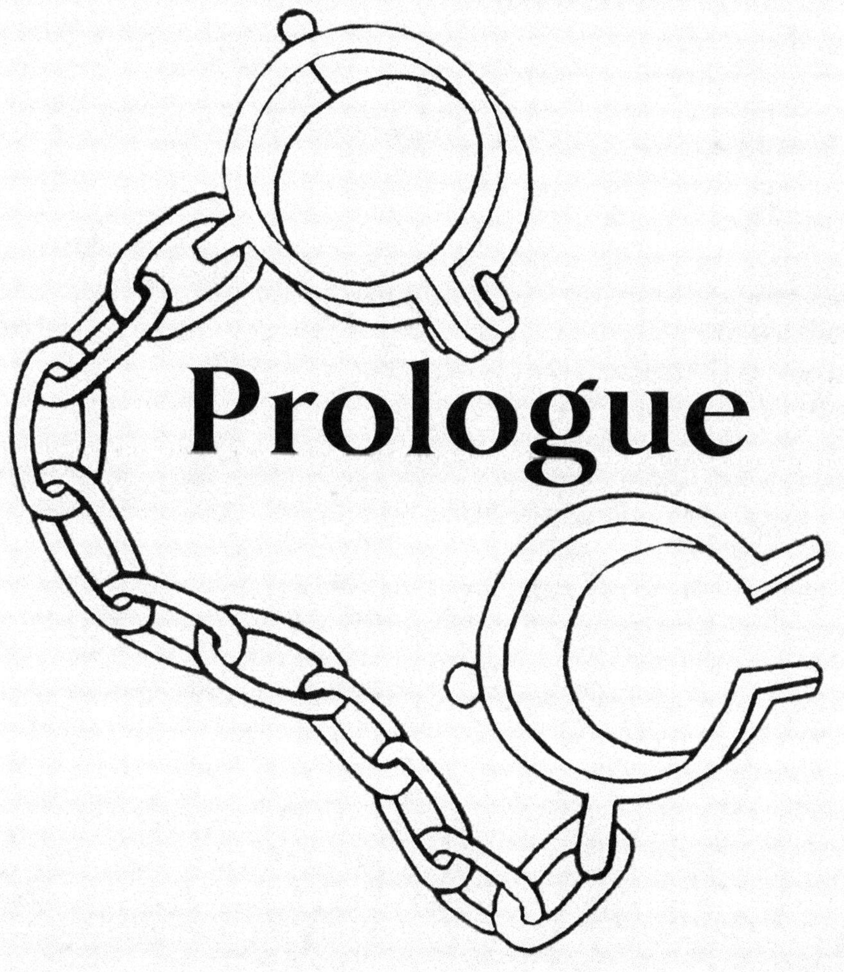

Mike Henry's fight to bury the ghost of chattel slavery in the Caribbean

It's 2021, centuries since British-sanctioned operatives led sleazy operations to raid areas in West Africa in search of human beings for capture and ultimate supply and sale as chattel slaves to fellow British subjects operating mostly sugar plantations in the Caribbean, including Jamaica.

Dragging their prey in large numbers from their abodes, Africans themselves, under economic arrangements with Europeans, especially the British, would arrange for the constant supply of 'human energy' of the repugnant kind for transfer by ship under utterly sub-human conditions to the Caribbean and North America as slaves and, even more critically, chattel or commodity, not people with any intrinsic value except for the labour which they were forced to provide.

No rights, no more relevance than any other item of property, such as cattle, horses or wagons, and like wild animals, herded around on economic agendas only, including for breeding purposes, again within the all-important economic focus that drove the colonial setting where sugar had become king of the hill, and a primary sustenance of the British Empire.

Amid the boom in Britain from the dastardly wrong implementation of the African slave trading system into the colonalised Caribbean and Americas for centuries, something which served to enrich the British Empire like other European powers over the period, the stain of the slave system wreaked havoc on the minds and capacities of the colonised societies across the Caribbean.

Essentially, to be black was to be part of the stock in trade within the British colonial system, where slavery over centuries deprived people of African ancestry and descent of the intrinsic human right to chart and determine their own fate or destiny.

Misused and abused, punished sometimes worse than any beast – even of burden – is normally treated, and butchered at times for any sign of dissent or defiance, the odds were so heavily stacked against members of the black race in the Caribbean during slavery, that even today, many descendants of the actual victims still bear the awful strain and stains of the human pilferage and degradation that the system entailed, and it will be quite some time before many are back on anything like even keel.

Indeed, black slaves had no value within the system of chattel slavery except for the processes of production and reproduction.

And almost two centuries after the forced abolition of the slave system, with Britain slowly and sparingly acknowledging the abominable wrong that slavery represented, but so far steering clear of similarly acknowledging responsibility for reparation to right the very pronounced and extended wrongs that were done, the fight continues in search of justice.

That fight has been long but sustained through a clear recognition that the goal is of critical importance to both the historical record of the Caribbean and the current realities that the region's development was significantly stymied by European colonialisation and exploitation, for which broad recognition and agreed reparation are must-have outcomes of the process, with question marks only applicable to when and what are to be involved in a settlement.

But for clarity, it is important to establish that in my case, as a forerunner in respect of the regional and national fight for reparation from Britain for the negative impact and exploitation of the transatlantic slave system, my central area of focus has been the fact of chattel slavery, not slavery in its varied and wider contexts that exists in different forms even today.

By definition, chattel slavery as was implemented by Britain and sustained for almost two centuries, involved enslaved persons who would supposedly be owned forever, and whose children and children's children would have been automatically enslaved.

Chattel slaves were individuals who were treated as complete property, to be bought and sold like any 'other' physical commodity, and were killed in many cases to keep others enslaved, something which was systematically sanctioned (made legal), implemented, operated and supported by some European governments and monarchs, including Britain.

Indeed, it should be noted, for example, that the White Anglo-Saxon Protestant movement in America historically sought to prove superiority and in the process, kill the minds and spirit of the black race with the adoption and promotion of the philosophy that being black represented evil.

So what has been done along the way of this sustained fight for reparation from Britain? Where is the fight now in terms of British and global response to the drive, and global justifications for the reparation cause?

Indeed, what of the decades-long fight for reparation and the justice that the nation and region stand to benefit so significantly from? This is where this publication is centred: the search by Mike Henry and others between 1980 and 2015 for a local political decision and the sustained fight for reparation for the injustices and exploitation of the British colonial slave system, which is a debt that is still owed to the descendants of the African slaves in the Caribbean.

Central to that drive was a series of Private Member's Motion that I tabled in the Jamaican Parliament in 2007, which, after clearing a number of stumbling blocks, ultimately got unanimous backing by the Members of the House in 2015.

The background to that motion was captured as follows in the 2013 publication of my book, 'Many Rivers to Cross'. The case for redress from Britain is based on the legal and moral consequences of enslavement and colonisation of individuals who were denied their fundamental rights and freedoms, including liberty, security of the person and the protection of the law, and suffered inhuman conditions without hope for relief.

Notably, the descendants of the enslaved persons were connected by ancestry of place of origin and race.

Also of note, the compensation that is being sought from Britain is due for the psychological and physical damage during the period of enslavement and all actions leading thereto or subsequent from that damage. Notably, this should all have been settled at the time of Jamaica's independence from Britain, but so long after, reparation and repatriation remain outstanding amid some major challenges on the global stage.

Before then, it was a tedious process to generate public support for reparation from Britain, this against significant resistance and even outright opposition from some quarters, including within the political sphere.

Indeed, for many years it was widely viewed that the fight for reparation was futile and not realistic, this amid a wall of silence from British leadership on the matter.

But over time that has changed somewhat with notably, former British Prime Minister Tony Blair, finally acknowledging the atrocities of the transatlantic slave trade and Britain's central role in it.

Interestingly though, Blair's concession came after he left office, and the critical apology to descendants of the slave population that is central to the reparation thrust, was not forthcoming from him, and has still not been tendered.

And in 2015, Blair's successor, Prime Minister David Cameron, came visiting Jamaica on an official visit, and incredibly, did not raise the subject of Jamaica and the region's ballooning claim for reparation from Britain over the two-day visit.

As should be expected, I, as a Member of the House of Representatives, declined to attend a House sitting in honour and recognition of Cameron's visit. My conscience and stomach just could not tolerate such wanton disregard for a nation, a region and a people which Britain had so wantonly exploited and abused while enriching itself in the process, yet does not want to discuss the matter at the governmental level in a frontal and firm way, which is the basic minimum platform that is acceptable in search of a resolution to the longstanding issue of the same kind of stain as apartheid, which can never be abandoned!

The circumstances of the visit represented an insult to, and a mockery of, our ancestors and our National Heroes who fought so hard against the historical oppression of our people.

Additionally, Cameron's visit to the Jamaican Parliament was within the context that the same Parliament had passed a motion years ago for reparation to be sought from Britain, but the subject matter was not on the House agenda for the visit by Cameron.

Additionally, it is to be noted that in the case of Cameron himself, the situation was even more sensitive, as history has revealed that ancestors of the then British Prime Minister actually owned slaves in the Caribbean centuries ago.

Britain's position has been in stark contrast to the reality that at the end of over 250 years of slavery in the Caribbean and the Americas in 1838, the European power paid a then very substantial sum of £20 million, 40 per cent of the British National Budget at the time, to the slave owners who lost their 'property', but no focus was seemingly then placed on compensation for the slaves themselves, and similarly none since then in relation to the gross negative consequences on the black population of the Caribbean region from the historical slur of the slave system.

Interestingly, this has been while compensation has been agreed to and undertaken, or is being negotiated, in respect of a number of far less negatively impactful atrocities across the globe, including in the United States, elsewhere in Europe and in the Middle East.[1]

Amid it all, there have been some fiery exchanges in the dialogue to fully establish both the national and regional positions, expectations and demands for reparation. Indeed, I can remember one such incident at a meeting at the Mona Campus of the University of the West Indies in May 2007. There I went ballistic like in the Black Lives Matter mode in response to the insensitivities that were coming from the then visiting Deputy Prime Minister of Britain, John Prescott.

---

1. Interestingly, historians have generally failed to realise and record that the United States of America was a colony like Jamaica, but while the other colonies experienced chattel slavery, the USA became the only colony in the Americas to have practised chattel slavery as a state-sanctioned and implemented aspect of its economic development.

With the high-level British representative simply echoing his leader Tony Blair's position of 'no apology', I promptly stormed out of the event, and pointedly asked the visiting official "How is it that you were prepared to pay the slave owners, but you are not willing to compensate the slaves?"

As I pay homeage to the Rastafarians who lived up to their motto of not giving up a continent for an island and seeking reparation which I maintain should be a part of the fight and settlement.

The 2007 debate in Parliament on the Private Member's Motion for reparation was an interesting exercise, the details of which are carried verbatim on a number of subsequent pages:

The Debate in Parliament (First Resolution)

Very few subjects will rile up my emotions as the need for reparation from some European nations for the atrocities that were committed during the period of slavery prior to its abolition in the 1830s.

Having long demonstrated my disgust at the absence of any constructive multilateral dialogue on the need for compensation for the descendents of the slave population (although the slave owners were summarily compensated for the loss of their 'human stock'), I took the challenge to the floor of the Jamaican Parliament in a Private Member's Motion in February 2007 while in Opposition.

The motion called for compensation in the form of cash or debt relief from the relevant European nations for the atrocities and abuse of the black population in the same way that, for example, the Jews were compensated for the Holocaust and the Maoris of New Zealand and the Japanese after World War 11.

Armed with my best deposition towards advocacy and broad understanding and appreciation of world history, I took the thorny global issue to the local Parliament in a most forceful manner, which culminated after a series of debates, with basically all my parliamentary colleagues then, ultimately joining in support of the motion.

A lifelong fighter for justice, I made it my purpose to mould in my colleagues the full relevance of the inhibiting effects of slavery on the development of the Caribbean region. Those, I urged, should be erased once and for all, through both the acceptance and implementation of a reparation agenda to remove the proverbial chip from the shoulders of the descendants of the black people who were transported in such indignity from Africa to the West Indies, and were subjected to degradation and wanton abuse at the hands of the slave masters.

And in recognition of our martyred heroes, both leaders and followers, like Sam Sharpe (a slave but a defined leader), George William Gordon and a whole slew of slaves like 'Tacky'.

To this day I am at a loss for words to explain how our leaders who led us into independence could not see that the first claim to independence has to be the settlement of brutality and the claim for exploited labour and ownership of land.

Indeed, in the 'Tacky' war, slaves were captured, tortured and executed on the spot, and some were roasted alive, with heads impaled on poles and bodies put on public display, and deportation to other islands was the order of the day.

So much so that revolts became endemic to Jamaica, which was seen as the colony that was most indispensable to the imperial prosperity and could quite justly represent the richest people in the entire British empire and by the late 18th century showed rates of return of 17 per cent annually on their investments.

The details of the debates in Parliament, which fell off the Order Paper in Parliament more than once, were as follows:

Mr. HENRY:

I want to thank my colleagues in the House for a matter that has long been near and dear to my political career, and one which engenders a great deal of passion.

Mr. Speaker, my Resolution says:

"WHEREAS the period of the slave trade was barbaric and uncivilised and represented one of the worst examples of man's inhumanity to man, and should not have been forgotten or repeated;

AND WHEREAS it was a direct consequence of this slave trade that the African people were scattered throughout the globe against their will;

AND WHEREAS this action led to the dismantling and the destabilisation of Africa so that children who were produced as a result have remained disenfranchised;

AND WHEREAS in direct proportion to the destabilisation of these sons and daughters was the growth and prosperity and power of the colonial masters;

AND WHEREAS the nations such as the English-speaking Caribbean which have evolved through wresting independence from their slave masters have remained doomed to be forever strangled by mushrooming debt;

AND WHEREAS history is replete with instances where compensation has been paid to nationalities for injustices and violations suffered, to wit, the Jews for the Holocaust, the Maoris of New Zealand and the Japanese after World War II;

AND WHEREAS it was unanimously passed in the House of Representatives of the 20th July, 1948, that all who desire to return to Liberia should be facilitated;

AND WHEREAS in response thereto, general instructions were issued to the then JLP Government on the 10th of June, 1964;

AND WHEREAS it is now 74 years since the Rastafari Brethren of Jamaica commenced the struggle for reparation and repatriation:

BE IT RESOLVED that this Honourable House, with a view to establishing a united and common position, debate the proposition that reparation is due to the countries of the displaced descendants."

I'm making an amendment to my Resolution, Mr. Speaker. And I'm taking out:

BE IT FURTHER RESOLVED that a committee of the House be established.

And I am asking that that be deleted. And in its place the second Prayer would substitute therefore the following:

"BE IT FURTHER RESOLVED that the Government accommodate any citizen or group of citizens who wishes to enter into dialogue on repatriation to Liberia, and to facilitate their request in accordance with the 1948 Resolution of this Honourable House."

And insert the word, and, before the final Prayer:

BE IT FURTHER RESOLVED that the nations due to make reparation be called upon to provide compensation by way of cash and/or debt relief.

(Dr. Harris applauds)

In my opening remarks, Mr. Speaker, the first reaction I know I will get is one of victim psychology. Let me dispense with that very early. And since it's Black History Month, since we are speaking on Bob Marley's birthday (February 4), I say that the mere fact that you wish to recall or commemorate, continues the perception of this syndrome and does not remove it.

Mr. Speaker, the Private Member's Motion which I have just read, speaks to matters that I have felt strongly about. Matters that are complex and which historically raise emotions previously not seen in even one of our closest friends and often times from the least expected quarters.

My own life experiences and observations in this matter, Mr. Speaker, are drawn from the travels I have made, the sojourns I've had throughout the world, North, South, East and West. But it remains fully rooted in my Jamaican ancestry and it is motivated by my quest for the answer as to why we are who we are today? And carries with it no less a revolutionary zeal than when I was a teenager.

For, Mr. Speaker, we are a country still in search of ourselves. And this search has one part of our history and descendancy responsible, while the other part keeps saying differently. And we therefore expound a forgive and forget structure, and a fear of appearing weak-kneed or as a mendicant. And then we speak of victim psychology.

But, Mr. Speaker, for me the Middle Passage was purely economics which carried with it racism, and this because the labour content was extracted from the black continent, the continent of the birth of civilisation. A continent which was easily exploitable and one which offered the white Anglo-Saxon Protestants a new way to economic growth and prosperity. Much has been made about the participated willingness in the economic development and the capturing of slaves by the Africans themselves. And it is saying that they willingly participated in the trade. Look at that, Mr. Speaker.

Mr. Speaker, that for me merely strengthens the case as it removes the racial overtones and expresses slavery for what it is, the economic exploitation of people.

People were used and abused so as to make the slave trading nations of Europe, Britain, France, Portugal, Netherlands and the Dutch, richer and richer, while the producers and the labourers were unjustifiably abused, murdered, raped, humiliated and treated as animals.

For that, Mr. Speaker, the British Government gave the slave traders and owners in the Caribbean compensation in payments of cash and land, and the abused were left to find their own way out of the psychologically-debilitating experience in a slow, painstaking formula of divide and rule, miscegenation, making those of us who look like the slave owners, that is the person of the mulatto status, take on the mantle of the slave owner...

Mr. PICKERSGILL:
Don't fool yourself.

Mr. HENRY:
Maybe I escaped, but I must claim that you can only be a Jew by your mother.

And relate in every way in that capacity to the field slaves, who remained at a secondary status until independence.

But then, Mr. Speaker, since independence has there been much change?

When independence came, Mr. Speaker, we spent little time looking at our history. For instance, the then Jamaican Government, if it had dealt with Rastafari as a cultural and religious movement and cited the indigenous claim of Rastafari, this would be a different Jamaica today. It could have done that and eased us all the pain, but it paid no attention to that aspect, while other countries emerging in their independence did so. Just as today we deal with other religions in the same way.

What we did then, Mr. Speaker, in reality, we buried our head in the sand, we sought to act as the house slaves were wont to do, hoping the matter would pass and we would be rescued by 'backra master', or indeed, the Lord would send us the messiah. But, Mr. Speaker, history does not go away. Indeed, history repeats itself, and if we fail to recall and remember history, then we are doomed to make the same mistakes again. It is therefore a conclusion of mine, Mr. Speaker, that we must, as a Parliament, seek out a revolution of the mind of the Jamaican. And so, Mr. Speaker, on this the 200th anniversary of the slave trade, and Bob Marley's birthday, I am pleased to speak on the matter, and I do so with the opportunity to air our feelings, not in commemoration, but in facing the realities of what we demand. We demand justice and an economic settlement, debt paid!

Mr. Speaker, I speak to this motion to have a political decision made. I repeat. A political decision made by an elected Parliament of an independent state and country, which boasts 90 to 95 per cent slave ancestry, a country which has proven its substantial commitment to democracy, but a country mired in debt and one which all but embraces anarchical tendencies and thinking; and dare I say it, Mr. Speaker, a country which in many ways still fosters and feeds the slave mentality as we fail to dignify with an identity, all our citizens, and we also

have failed for each of us to take responsibility for our future. This is manifested today, Mr. Speaker, and contained in the lack of respect for our women and the feeding of the irresponsibility of manhood and fatherhood.

Mr. Speaker, did not the slave owners brand the slaves with a hot iron like how they do the cattle in the west? Does this not beg the question as to whether this is or may be the cause why we now shy away from the identity of our citizens in every form. And we continue to use aliases instead of a pride in our names, as we then did to escape from one plantation to the next, breeding each other for the benefit of backra master.

Mr. Speaker, in all of my research, and I stand to be corrected, for indeed I am a babe in the woods in this matter, a matter which more learned and eminent men have tackled, some to no avail. I can find nowhere, Mr. Speaker, where a sovereign Parliament which has suffered from slavery has voted on the entitlement of reparation, and I demand from my Parliament such a decision.

(Applause)

For as I said, Mr. Speaker, in my research I have seen debates, arguments, lawsuits and conferences, all to the highest judicial and intellectual levels. But I have not found one which reflects a vote for a decision by an elected Parliament, which has either accepted or rejected reparation. A decision which if made by a government would, I feel, sanction the pursuance of this matter to the highest world court, and have that world court either reject the justified plea or accept it.

Instead, Mr. Speaker, I feel that we have resiled from the political decision, and have allowed the lead to be taken by individuals and organisations of legal minds, many of whom are our own Jamaicans.

Recently, Mr. Speaker, I have seen increasing apologies from heads of states – I am asked to spare the Queen in this presentation.

Dr. HARRIS:

She benefitted the most.

Mr. HENRY:

I think – it is unparliamentary, they tell me – to deal with an abstract leadership which is not fully recognised in my own personal needs.

Recently, Mr. Speaker, we have seen increasing apologies from heads of states, monarchs and presidents. I have no problem with accepting or receiving apologies, which by their very issuance carry with them guilt and responsibility.

But for me, Mr. Speaker, that is not good enough, as it must carry with it compensation equal to the act. And I daresay that the recent price paid by the leader of Iraq shows how strong nations feel when illegal acts are carried out on the innocent and unsuspecting, and against their will.

Mr. Speaker, over the history of man we have seen the need to revisit acts of history and attempt to rectify wrongs and crimes committed against humanity. And I would have then again read all that I have read, which is here, but I will put it into the context of the presentation. Because, Mr. Speaker, this has been acted on and echoed by voices for and voices against.

And, Mr. Speaker, in 1992, Chief Abiola instigated the creation of the OAU Group of Imminent Persons for Reparation, among them was our own Dudley Thompson, who should be congratulated for being a part of that.

(Applause)

Mr. Speaker, that paper is entitled '*Political versus legal strategies for the African slaverly reparation movement*'. I had planned to circulate this to the press, Mr. Speaker, but I am going to leave them to go on the internet because I haven't seen much reported in the press about this debate. I have seen many things reported on from Parliament of what was taking place. You see us quarreling amongst ourselves, but the reality and the sense of whom or what we are hasn't even been reported. I quote:

I do not dispute that harm has been inflicted upon Africans both in Africa and in the Americas because of the slave trade.

When harm has been inflicted, a cause of action can be

created in the law for the satisfaction of that claim of harm. Reparation have been paid for the harm inflicted on a class or race of people. For example, since World War II, Germany has paid at least 88 billion Deutsche Marks in reparation to the state of Israel...

And in case we think that ended a long time ago, they were to pay another 20 billion in the year 2005, that was two years ago. I am not going to go to the United States Government in relation to what they paid to the Japanese, because, as I said, that is what is obfuscating a lot of settlement, that we must identify who were born as African slaves. **I am not saying anything must go to the individual, it must go to the state,** and I will prove that by how it went to the Israeli estate. But, indeed, Mr. Speaker, presently the Chinese have discussed the possibility of suing the Government of Japan for the atrocities committed during the capture of the city of Nanking, which resulted in the systematic murder of more than 300,000 Chinese by Japanese soldiers during World War II. 'Comfort women' from Korea who were forced into prostitution during World War II by the Japanese, have similarly organised to sue the Government of Japan for reparation. I go on, Mr. Speaker.

Quoting from the OAU document:

The question before us is whether the African slavery reparation movement should pursue legal paths or political paths.

I know legal paths have been sought. I am hoping to direct the Government to go about it, but the political path has never been decided on.

Perhaps both paths may be pursued. Among the questions to be addressed are the advantages and disadvantages of both approaches.

Mr. Speaker, I seek the political path to engender the legal path. I go on, Mr. Speaker.

Reparation for damages done to a race of people have precedents in international, German, and American law.

The question then becomes how the African reparation movement can pursue this claim.

And the article goes on.
It would seem that the interested parties in reparation would have a claim that needs satisfaction. The next set of questions then involve the venue of the suit and the question of whether a statute of limitations applies.

And I hope to prove that the statutes of limitations do not apply, because I hope in the end to prove that the Nuremberg trial, from which they were extracted and the trial of Germany could not have related and would have affected that aspect.
First, it would obviate the necessity and costs of suing in the separate courts of England, France, Spain, Portugal and the Netherlands. Second, fixing the venue of the lawsuit in an international court (like the International Court of Justice) would give it maximum international media exposure.
I go on to a very important section.
The question for us in the African Slavery Reparation movement is whether our efforts to obtain reparation should involve political or legal tactics to obtain our objectives.

And that clearly is a position that we must look at and, therefore, as it states here:
We also need to examine whether the venues for our political and legal efforts should take place in international or national arenas.

For my part, Mr. Speaker, I expect it to take part in the international arena, and I recommend to anyone, and I circulate this for copying, the African Studies Quarterly of the online Journal for African studies, Political versus legal strategies for the African Slaverly Reparation Movement.
And so, Mr. Speaker, I wish to move chronologically, because

that is a few years old, that is 1992. But in 2002, some 10 years later, to show the matter is still alive, I quote from ***N. COBRA, All things deep***. And I will quote the part that speaks to the psyche.

> *The impact of slavery is hard to deny. The current value of slave labor is estimated at $1.4 trillion, and as many as 28 million lives were affected by the slave trade, forming the basis for economic, cultural and political disparities present in much of West Africa and black America. That includes the existence of...*

Which I don't need to speak to, of white privilege, a belief system that began during slavery and continues; one which alienates our religious beliefs, or the African religious beliefs, the impossibility of us to face our Africanism, the impossibility of us wanting to recognise that we all came from that aspect of our history, because it suits us to bleach ourselves and escape the reality of who we are.

(Applause)

Mr. HENRY:

And so I am moving, Mr. Speaker, to prove the aspect of business, because I am going now to May 2002, Mr. Speaker. I am going to California, where they are considering slavery operations, and they are considering it from a State that never allowed slaves. So it is as current as anything else. And I bring this up because it speaks to the economics, because I don't want to get embroiled into the internal strife of the black American against the regime of the United States, which gained its economic growth from slavery. That's an internal matter. I am dealing with it from a Jamaican stand point. But for businesses, let us understand, and I quote – ***"California never allowed slaves, but it may become the first state in the nation to make slave reparation a reality".***

Two years ago, Democratic Governor Rae Davis signed a law forcing insurance companies to disclose policies they wrote for slave owners more than a century ago. This week the States

Department of Insurance released the information. None of the half dozen insurance companies are based in California, but they all did business in the State. I ask for that smoking gun to be established against maybe some of our very insurance companies that exist today, and whether they in fact didn't insure the slave owner against the loss of his slaves. Was that not economics? In any event, last week Governor Davis said he would be interested in making amend if insurance companies did profit from slavery. *"Clearly we want to right any wrongs and do justice to people who are taken advantage of"*, he told an audience of digital connection in conference.

I would like to laud Governor Davis for his enlightened approach to this matter.

(Applause)

But in order to balance it, Mr. Speaker, I have in my hand ***'Slavery Reparation – A Misguided Movement'***, by a Professor Peter Schuck, Yale Law School, jurist guest lumnist. His argument, Mr. Speaker, as is the argument of those who face it, is around instrumental consequentialist and, as he states, horizontal equity, and I bring it between what is simply put, his instrumentalist objectives. All, of course, meant to confound, confuse and escape the reality of what it is.

His consequential argument held by many is again another smoke screen. Because, and I quote from him:

"First, how would it define the beneficiary class?"

Need I go much more?

"Would it include all blacks in the US, all of those descending from slaves? What about immigrant blacks and how would 'black' be defined in an increasingly multi-racial society? If the latter, what about descendants of the blacks? Second, how would the beneficiaries prove their entitlement? Absent is a clear definition of black and who would judge."

I think I hear one of my colleagues wonder if I am black. But, Mr. Speaker, as a mulatto (Jew), I learned to be black when I tried to struggle in the white man's world and I wasn't employed because I didn't have his degree. But I will deal with that at another time. It certainly brought me down to ground anyway.

"Third, would beneficiaries have to show that American slavery caused their current condition? And, four, should all taxpayers bear the cost?

Now, Mr. Speaker, all I am saying is, I don't want you to pay every individual. I want you to pay the Jamaican Government for the Jamaican Government to implement and utilise what is due theirs for the labour that was done by the worker and, therefore, pay it to the State.

And let me point this out, because clearly he goes on under consequentalist objections, and he answers his own self because what does he say? *"The Post World War II reparation that Germany paid to Israel, although criticised by many as insulted and inadequate 'blood money', were far more successful, and helped the launch of the new State"*. Is it because we are black we must be separated now? Although I would like to remind them the Falasha-Jews were the first Jews in the world and they were black.

He goes on to say, *"The most attractive model for black reparation is the programme for Japanese interned during World War II"*, an American position, obviously. But then he really speaks and he equally tries in his horizontal equity to even involve our own Orlando Patterson's quote in which *"Hitler's willing executioners argue that even slaves were treated as socially dead than Jews were in Germany during the Nazi period"*. But, Mr. Speaker, where I think he defeats (himself) and, as he puts it, he cites for me the case of the American Indians. But need I say that the American Indians were given their reservations and their lands and were given their internal aspect of control and government. So I ask how plural is it? Rather than, he states, *"that the politics of psychology of the competition for victimhood will make it difficult to stop there and that every effort to justify the stopping point will arouse new bitterness and magnify existing feelings."*

Mr. Speaker, I put this position where I think it belongs, either in file 13 or in the dump bin, which merely seeks to insult the intelligence of every person who knows what slavery meant or didn't mean to the world. But by him, even in that article, he also went to 9/11 and Oklahoma City to seek reparation. I reject it when he asked in that *article if slavery is the greatest injustice. I say yes! I say it as it relates to our world, and I state that it is the greatest injustice to man.*

And so, Mr. Speaker, I move to 2004, December 6 to 7, to be exact, in the session of the 'Consultative Assembly of Parliamentarians for the International Criminal Court and the Rule of Law'. And I do so, Mr. Speaker, because in the course of this debate I need to hear from the Government side what is our present position on the Statute of Rome, and where we as a country stand on this, because of some of the things I will say and have said.

It is worthy to note here that neither the United States nor Iraq has ratified the Rome Statute. For the purpose of this statute, let me cite – and I trust my legal friends will assist – Crime Article No.7 states,

"Crime against humanity means any of the following acts when committed as a part of a widespread or systematic attack directed against any civilian population with knowledge of the attack. It includes murder, extermination, enslavement, deportation, imprisonment, torture, rape, persecution, enforced disappearance of persons, the crime of apartheid and other inhumane acts".

When the phrase "crimes against humanity" was used, Mr. Speaker, in the Nuremberg Trials in 1945, the convening nations did not bother to explain what gave them the right to define and punish such crimes. It was presumed as self-evident that certain actions were so terrible that they must be treated as illegal, even if they might have been permissible under Nazi German law when they took place. The so called "Rome Statute" which created the international criminal court in the Hague in 2002, specifically defines crimes against humanity in terms drawn from the Nuremberg Charter. And the definition used by the Iraqi Special Tribunal was copied from there, as recent as now. For the record, let me note again, that neither Iraq nor America has signed the Statute of Rome. And recently you have seen it used in the case against Saddam Hussein. **I claim, Mr. Speaker, that the claim against the slave traders is far more heinous, than any act against humanity carried out by anyone else and the horror of the atrocities is known.**

(Applause)

And, Mr. Speaker, I am not asking for the death penalty, I am asking for reparation to the country in cold, hard cash and debt relief.

(Applause)

I wish to ask the legal fraternity to use the legitimacy of the International Law to prove that slavery was one of the crimes against humanity, which, by the way, in the Nuremberg trial were the same nations which did not even bother to explain what gave them the right to define and punish such crimes. How then now? But it was accepted as self-evident that certain actions were so terrible that they must be treated as illegal even if they might have been permissible under Nazi law, a position still held by the slave trading countries.

And so, Mr. Speaker, I will draw attention to that December 6 third session of the Consultative Assembly of Parliamentarians for the International Criminal Court and the Rule of Law, December 6, 2004, which examined these things and included a number of parliamentarians from across the world. And I will quote from Mr. H.E.C.M. Ter Braack, Ambassador from the Netherlands to New Zealand, who spoke on behalf of the presidents of the European Union, while Mr. Jonas Sjostedt – I don't know if I am pronouncing their names right – addressed the participants on behalf of the PGA Group of the European Parliament, and it goes on to assess the approach that should be taken in promoting the universality of the Rome Statute, and the universality of that implementation. And I will circulate this for everyone to look at because this is a course of action – and the Government must tell me, are we going to look at the statute in Article 7? Are we going to begin to cite these as part of the way forward?

If indeed, Mr. Speaker, the countries responsible for the slave trade, the British, the French, the Dutch, the Portugese are not willing to sit down at the table and take responsibility for the act and approach a settlement in real economic terms in much the same way as they settled with slave owners, **then I call on us Parliamentarians to seek reparation in the highest courts of justice, and receive on behalf of descendants of us the slave servants that which was given to the slave masters, amounts in cash and equity equal to the barbaric act of slavery. Barbaric acts, which I am sure colleagues will reiterate, but which I repeat, I will name** but a few:

- Φ murder; the tossing of persons into the sea merely for economic gain and because they wish to escape the law, for it limited the amount of slaves you could carry, and if they came to investigate it, you just pushed the people overboard and left them to drown in the sea;

- Φ extermination: the decimation of thousands and thousands of persons in pursuant of economic gain;

- Φ enslavement: the holding of persons against their will for economic gains;

- Φ deportation: the scattering of tribes and individuals across the globe for economic gains;

- Φ torture: the beatings and incarceration of persons against their will for economic gains;

- Φ rape: the defilement of our women bought and sold as chattels and expected to bow to their masters' wish; the miscegenation of a people for economic and psychological enslavement, all for economic gains; enforced disappearance of people, abandoned, discarded and buried without a trace in the pursuit of economic growth and gain.

Mr. Speaker, we will never be able to place the real value on these barbaric acts, but our ancestors cry out from their graves for justice. And who could readily deny that our own recent upsurge in blood-letting may not be the cry from the grave. It certainly speaks to a gap in the psyche of our people. I have not asked, nor have I seen any need to really rally anyone to the cause which many others have sought long before I make this move. For my part, I feel the matter touches us all and goes to the heart of who or what we are.

So whether reparation comes in the form of payments tied to infrastructure or education, I ask today that we as a Parliament decide what we feel is just. Let us clearly stake out our position on slavery and its impact on our lives. I again state that for me, truth and reconciliation goes further than mere words, and if this was not so, then the very countries who were dodging the issue should not seek a resolution when it affects their own or their countries psyche and speak to another in respect of Jamaica.

I have seen and recognised the internal struggle of the US blacks for their own government to respond to their suffering as a result of their own government's actions and all its racial implications. **For our part, let us act as a country and take our stand for justice as Jamaicans and let it ring like the bell of freedom, freedom from the abuse of the past. Let us seek the compensation to lift the veil of irresponsibility of the individual once known as 'boy' or with an alias.**

Compensation to be used to return dignity to our women and men who were treated as productive animals, and let us as a Parliament, if victorious in reducing the burden of our debt, call on the wisdom of Solomon to act in the interest of a country and a people who may have missed opportunities due in no small way to a debilitated psyche caused by abuse and deliberate acts of man's inhumanity to man. And let us seek to build with it a society where no citizen is left behind.

In closing this section of my presentation, Mr. Speaker, I must also speak as it relates to the repatriation movement so ably advocated over the years by that body of persons of Rastafari **'livity'**, and I seek from the government a decision on this matter. I refer to the repatriation and the decision of the House in 1948, and the perpetuity of that commitment as I will hope in closing, to speak to many other aspects of it.

I trust that I have dealt with this matter with the passion and the feeling and the reality with which I think it relates, and I sincerely hope that as we address it – I don't wish to call for a divide, but I would like to see a vote for everyone as to how do we think we must pursue reparation in the interest of our country as a repayment for all the suffering and pain which can never ever be valued, but in the reality of the moment that is damaged which our psyche left us divided, which left us in many ways unable to capitalise on the true reality and the spirit of whom we are.

I trust that I will get the support in the context of this presentation and that we look forward to a brighter day as we debate, for me, this very important subject.

Thank you very much.

(Applause)

Note: After other contributions Mr. Henry closes.

Mr. HENRY:

The fact that this debate has gone on for three days, and for which a number of people still yearn to speak, proves that what it lacked all along was political decisions and political leadership. Because, indeed, as I said and I think that I am not wrong in quoting it, that I'm prepared to stand alone. I have waited and I've seen no action. I pointed out that there was a missing link and that that missing link, was, and I will quote from my speech because I don't wish to go over and over what we should have known so long ago. And indeed my colleague who sits beside me is not here, but I am always tempted to just sit down and say, I rest my case. But, Mr. Speaker, what has been read, what has been said, is the additional aspect to my appeal for a political decision on the basis that all that we have heard proves that it has affected the psyche of our people. And so let me repeat from my speech.

But, Mr. Speaker, for me the Middle Passage slavery, and I emphasise the Middle Passage slavery, when I close I will show the historical context of the Maoris that slavery was a system that existed, that indeed, through the Arabs it had a different name and connotation in its social structure, and therefore slavery has existed and will continue to exist. And I dare say in modern times some of our helpers are still going through slavery right now.

Mr. DALLEY:
Some of our who?

Mr. HENRY:
Helpers at home. Because remember, I'm speaking to the psyche of Jamaica standing alone. Remember it was Jamaica who stood alone against apartheid.

Mr. BUCHANAN (LUTHER):
Hear, hear.

Mr. HENRY:
Remember it was Bustamante who said I stand with the West making a decision. I have said ...

GOVERNMENT MEMBERS:
Hear, hear, hear, hear.

Mr. HENRY:
I have said, I don't want to go through why Bustamante was thrown out of his own father's home to live on a hill because he married black. I don't want to go there because I don't want the race aspect to emanate in this. Because we mustn't allow the Anglo-Saxon Protestants who entered this whole aspect of slavery and influenced the psyche and the divide and rule, to continue to divide and rule. So let me speak to what I said.

"For me the Middle Passage slavery was purely economics which carried with it racism, and this because the labour content was extracted from the black continent, the continent of the birth of civilisation, a continent which was easily exploitable for economic purposes, and for which it participated willingly in the economic gain of capturing the slaves. "So my focus," I continued, "is blinkered and narrow. It is economics. It certainly isn't the aspect of all the other obfuscation, because if Nigeria speaks, Nigeria speaks because they may have to pay for slavery internally."

A MEMBER:
True.

Mr. HENRY:
And I emphasise quite clearly that I don't wish to talk about who inherited or didn't inherit, I said it should be given to the State. And I said Jamaica should be prepared to go it alone. For indeed, as I said, the slave traders and owners of Jamaica were compensated by their governments in payments of cash and land and the precedent exists. The lawyers can take it from there. You can take that twenty million and you can work that twenty million out. But as long as we continue to allow the obfuscation of every possible situation to influence this, then we certainly will not move forward. Therefore, what I ask for, what I remind Parliament is what has been missing, a political decision by a politically elected Parliament that is answerable to the people who elected it.

So that Jamaica, if it has to fight it alone, should do so. For my part as a Private Member's Motion, I intend to fight it in every corner from here on and every chance I can speak, and I am willing to take it to the street to the people for their own comments.

So I quote:

'I seek this motion to have a political decision made by a duly elected Parliament of an independent State and country which boasts a 90 - 95 per cent slave ancestry. A country which has proven its substantial commitment to democracy, a country mired in debt and one which all but embraces anarchical tendencies and thinking.'

And I went on to say, and I want to repeat it:
'A country which in many ways still fosters and feeds the slave mentality. A country which in many ways we fail in dealing with our identity as citizens, and therefore we fail to take responsibility for ourselves.'

I don't think that could be any plainer in terms of the purpose that I intended for this Bill.

Mr. HENRY:
So, Mr. Speaker, the path I trod is deliberately so. I almost started the speech by saying, I greet you in the name of Jah Rastafari. It's a path trod by many before me, and I will refer to some of them.

Thanks to all of those who have participated, Mr. Speaker, inspired by much of the comments. But let me again pay tribute to the pioneers. And the economics of slavery in the middle passage must not be confused with race, racial walls, tribal wars and should be seen for what it is.

So, Mr. Speaker, sitting in the gallery, I want to be recognised specifically, Mr. Philmore Alvaranga and Mr. Moses Nelson, and I think we deserve to give them a round of applause.

(Applause)

Because this didn't start last year or with my motion. I have in my hand a letter to Her Majesty, Queen Elizabeth, dated 1961. I have in my hand a copy to the Rt. Honourable Harold Macmillan. May I point out to you that he was the one who talked about the 'wind of change' that was, sweeping the world.

(Sotto voce comment by Government Member)

Mr. HENRY:
1961. I have in my hand a letter from the United Nations to them in July 2002, replying to their letter of April 26, 2002. And I am going to put all of these for I hope Hansard to record.

Mr. Speaker, I have in my hand a letter from the Public Record Office and the National Archives of Great Britain to the same Mr.

Alvaranga, signed by a Mr. Nick Wood, of a project, which related to how we deal with registration of ourselves. Funny enough, Mr. Speaker, I have from them in 2002, 'Blair discusses African development with regional leaders', which speaks to some of what we are speaking to here. And then, Mr. Speaker, this one I will have to read, this is from 10 Downing Street. It is addressed to the Rastafari Brethren of the Reparation Association of Jamaica.

"The Prime Minister has asked me to thank you ...

This is Prime Minister Blair.

...for your recent letter. Mr. Blair would like to reply personally, but as you will appreciate, he receives many thousands of letters each week and this is not possible.

The matter you raise is the responsibility of the Foreign and Commonwealth Office, therefore, he has asked that your letter be forwarded to that department, so that they may reply to you on his behalf".

(Sotto voce comment by Government Member)

Mr. HENRY:

That's the same gentleman, Tony Blair. And I have letters of other people who have signed in terms of it. But that's the same gentleman who later on is apologising in 2006, three years later. Three years later, regrets on reparation.

The sting of that insult from my end, Mr. Speaker, I reject in every sense of the word. It speaks to the psyche of the persons who have perpetuated slavery, benefitted from slavery and continued by their aspect of divide and rule, to exploit that very thing in the essence of this very Parliament that we are part of.

But he says Jamaica need not be begging for aid, but a proud nation which was wronged, and which demands compensation. In fact, really this is Anthony Gifford's article of Blair's apology.

I read all of that, Mr. Speaker, to try and begin to put this in the context of the Middle Passage, in the context of what Jamaica has to deal with, and what Jamaica is suffering from. And if the others don't wish to join us, are we saying that if we don't have them coming with us we have resiled ourselves to being cowards, afraid to face the world and afraid to say to the world, to the Spanish, the British, the Dutch, the French, that we demand reparation for the act that it is.

(Applause)

Mr. Speaker, the article from the Economist of '07 – I will just read a few quick parts. "Such misery was found in a global trading system that in its heyday in the mid-18th Century was taking 85,000 Africans across the Atlantic – It's the Middle Passage I speak to – to work on sugar and tobacco plantations.

At one point the plantations of San Domique provided two thirds of France's overseas wealth. By the mid-18th century though, Britain was the biggest slave trading nation, and ports like Bristol, Liverpool and London thrived as a result.

Mr. Speaker, I am talking economics. I am talking about being paid for our productive labour which was exploited by whatever means, taken and used to build Britain and all the European countries, for which they have left us divided with a psyche in our ...

(Applause)

Mr. Speaker, the wounds of slavery are still too raw to be exposed in public. This is the Economist's article. Even more so is the stigma of slavery and it remains attached to slave dependants, who in some cases still cannot inherit property.

Mr. Speaker, do we think that all this capturing of land and this land that's owned in Jamaica that suddenly everybody owns, is not part of that whole psyche of development, historical, cultural, social and political? If I speak with passion, I speak with the passion of seeing my country at the point of where it is.

And so, Mr. Speaker, we have heard names mentioned and I am paying respect to the pioneers, Mrs. Blake-Hanna, Dr. Verene Shepherd chairing the bicentennial committee; Lord Gifford, and they all provided me before I close with different aspects, which I hope the House will allow me not to read into, but offer to be put into the records in the essence of time.

Culpability of the Spanish, Portugese, Americans and Dutch in the trans-Atlantic slave trade dissemination of the indigenous populations. For it didn't only begin, Mr. Speaker, with bringing slaves. And perhaps it's an escape of paying for the Tainos and the others that the Spanish completely eliminated from our psyche, that we want to forget it all.

I am never one to say that because I murdered someone it means it isn't murder. In 1550, the Spanish issued the first Assiento licences to the Portugese to trade enslaved Africans to replace the slaughtered indigenous labour force.

Mr. Speaker, there will be a committee of the House to which all of this will be presented. I am saying it in the context of the people who have offered the information. I am saying that we don't need to re- plough old ground. We need to chart new waters for a beginning and an inspiration that moves Jamaica in the right direction.[2]

(Applause)

So, Mr. Speaker, the legal basis of the claim for reparation, I could never handle it as Lord Anthony Gifford, British Queens Counsel and Jamaican attorney-at-law did. His presentation in all areas are here and I trust Hansard will absorb it as I pass it to them. But let me quote:

"Claims have been made, not only by descendants, but by the nation state which has had to bear the burden of paying for the consequences of the crime. As noted above."

---

2. It should be noted that the House committee that was agreed to in principle, was never appointed.

And we must not let this escape us, because if we mention the Nuremberg trial, if we mention the recent trial of Saddam Hussein, if we feel that the aspect of saying that the law existed to allow you to deal with slaves is irrelevant! Because what it has said is, if you knowingly commit that act, no matter at what time – because, indeed, Mr. Speaker, it is what the German generals sought to hide by in the trial for the Jews. They said it was an order from Hitler for them to burn all the Jews!

So are we saying that since it's an order of Queen Victoria – as noted above, for is it not so that Israel successfully claimed reparation from West Germany for the cost of resettling Jewish refugees, even though the State of Israel ... And Mr. Speaker, I can connect that because when I connect it to the Maoris, to the Arabs, to the Jews when slavery and black was just a part of the dictionary before the Anglo-Saxon Protestants introduced the racial context within it, then we'll begin perhaps to understand where we are heading.

Mr. Speaker, I am going to quote from the number of claims that would be assessed by experts in each aspect of life, each region affected by the institution of slavery. This may answer a lot of what others are questioning. I don't think I need to read them all, they are a learned opinion – as I said in my earlier presentation, intellectuals and all the various areas have discussed this matter. I can't distill and speak to what already exists. What we need to do is to seek to have the guts to understand. Because, you know, Mr. Speaker, some of it will come out here. There was a time when I was really totally proud to be a Jamaican. And I hope within my speech I can speak to this fact, the fact of the English who used to say to me, but you are not Jamaican, how you speak such good English. And my retort was, I picked it up on the boat coming over.

(Laughter)

Mr. Speaker, one grows up to hopefully emerge from a system which perpetuates the concept of the denigration of some persons by their descendancy as was stereotyped by the Anglo-Saxon Protestants who made it racial. I know what it is to look for the flame of justice to burn. So today, Mr. Speaker, we continue as a country to fight and resist the African influence, rather than placing it in its honest historical,cultural and social place. So we fight patois. I heard my colleague say why do we need patois. I can bring material here to prove to you that patois is as structured a language as was old English. They forget if Chaucer's tales were put to us in the way it was written, none of us would be able to understand it and read it. Why? Is it because patois emanates from a method of correspondence between Jamaicans seeking to communicate, to keep their identity, that because we are who we are, patois must be sacrificed?

How are we going to deal with it now, Mr. Speaker? Each of us speak and I can speak English in the most brilliant way, but I certainly do not communicate that way with my colleagues. So, Mr. Speaker, what are we going to do? Tell England now they can't hire the interpreter for the courts, where the Jamaicans who have left are facing the courts and are speaking their own language which the English court does not understand? Are we aware they are now paying people to interpret in the United Kingdom courts when a Jamaican is charged? In fact, I look on that as an economic way of growth because certainly, I could make some money in England being the interpreter for a court, and therefore benefit from the cultural, social and historical context in which I grew.

Let me remind the House, Mr. Speaker, Bob Marley wasn't recognised by us until the outside world recognised him, no matter how we wish to seek to quote it. And indeed, there are certain things which did not matter to this country until they came above Half-Way Tree or affected us individually. How easily could we really find out if Marcus Garvey formed the first political party? Perhaps if he wasn't as black as he was, he may have had the most successful political party. But he transformed trade unionism, which he didn't see as our way forward, and went into politics, which he saw as the way forward.

Mr. Speaker, I believe each of us has had our Waterloo; and as we now hopefully together share a path, I remind us that the forces that were unleashed for the abolition of slavery were not expected to succeed, but they did succeed. Am I to be left committed to myself, or am I to feel that because Barbados, Trinidad, Guyana, Cayman are not with me, I can't succeed? Am I to understand that I must rest the case?

Government:
No way.

Mr. HENRY:
Am I to understand that because Nigeria was part of the slave trade, I have in my hand the 'Iron Thorn'? This is the defeat of the British by Jamaican Maroons, the early masters of guerilla warfare. History is written, but probably not used in our schools. But, Mr. Speaker, this was the first defeat of the British. We criticised the Maroons without crediting the Maroons with the fact that if you sign a treaty which says you must protect your borders and you must co-operate with those who have surrendered to you like the British, are we now saying that because the Maroons returned slaves, they shouldn't be a part of it? It is almost the same as the argument I hear, that because everybody does it, we shouldn't be claiming.

Mr. HENRY:
Mr. Speaker, there is a saying, time heals all wounds, and this will apply to slavery in its literal sense. For I am sure that the scars of the whipped have been healed by death, as also the bleeding wounds and indeed the tears have all been dried. But the habits of survival and the planned divide and rule continue to affect how we think, how we move and have our being and they still exist today.

There are many talk-show hosts who feel that after 200 years we should have dealt with slavery, and if we haven't, then whose fault? That, of course, speaks to governance, Mr. Speaker, and the system of governance. It speaks to our leaders who, in my view, up to now have still not faced many of these realities. And I agree that one such is the responsibility for self and for our own actions. Since then, and I dare say that such failed action is to demand reparation. It's to demand it and to explain it to all the people of

Jamaica that they can understand who we are, why we are.

On the subject, I am told we should proceed cautiously as it still takes time. Mr. Speaker, all of us, including you, who came from the psyche of divide and rule, the we and they, the black, the brown, the psyche of divide, of being able to read and write. Because, Mr. Speaker, we must remember, adult suffrage came, because at one time who wanted to rule the people, if they didn't own land, they couldn't vote, and if they couldn't read and write they couldn't vote. I don't know what sounded more like a slave master running his own people than what existed. And it becomes a daily fight after 200 years later for us to promote this matter and confront it.

Thus, Mr. Speaker, I have chosen to speak on the economics and the rest I wanted to leave to the historians and the intellectuals. So I focussed on the strictest of economic terms, just payment for labour, abuse of power, which came out of economic exploitation. If Jamaica was to be paid what it is due for our productive labour in cash and debt relief, this would unleash for the development, sums large enough to transform and re-engineer our social landscape. What is required is wise leadership in the administration.

Mr. Speaker, I learnt to confront it when I left on a banana boat with my then wife to study in the UK. There was no room in the inn and the sign said no black people. I left here thinking being brown, I could escape, but I slept often on the street. No jobs for you. You weren't educated in England. Thank God, Mr. Speaker, I participated in the Nottinghill Gate riots to compensate for my own feeling in that period of time when the first riots took place in Nottinghill Gate against this system to break down the barriers, that we could sleep in rooms like everybody else.

Mr. BUCHANAN (LUTHER):
Hear, hear.

Mr. HENRY:
Mr. Speaker, if I give you the story of what it was, because when I went to school – and I am sure some of us have been – I remember being called a "reddibo". I never knew what this was.

But I am a proud man today because I can say to the black people there was a tribe of Hebrews that were red. So when we even talk about slavery and colour and race, and as I will come to prove, in fact black is considered so pure in the Arabic/Israeli world that it was considered the purity of colour. So if we deal with this, we have to deal with the historical psyche and the realities which address us, and let our children know what it is. Mr. Speaker, for instance, big businesses are built on specific analysis of needs. Fulfilling these needs, predicting those strengths and capitalising on them.

And why do I raise that, Mr. Speaker. I raise that because we believe the sugar thing came about just by fun. We forgot that in England in those days, it was still cold, wet and damp weather; that in fact the aspect of sugar being taken in the body generated heat, and that the more sugar you had in relation to it, the more you could withstand not having anything to heat the rooms you lived in. Do we want to go onto Coca Cola? Do we want to go on to the fact that the Coca Cola drink was an analysis of what it is that the human body could take, which after 10 days it will become addicted to, so Coca Cola was mixed with arsenic and cocainc, and then moved to caffeine? Do I need to move to the tobacco industry? Do we forget the ads that used to say "give me the 10- day test for a cigarette"? I used to have a story I exchanged with a very good [late] friend of mine, who I wish to record right now. His name is [was] Scully Scott.[3] And I used to remember what we said was we always pictured six young men in tennis gear playing tennis upstate New York at six in the evening – this was just when computers came in – they would jump in their limousine come down to Fifth Avenue, go up to the 13th floor to a bank of computers – you know one time computers used to be half of this room – and they would go in there and they would punch into the computer what rainfall would take place in the Caribbean, how much wind would blow across the desert, blowing whatever winds to affect you, how it would affect the coffee crop and the cocoa crop; and then they would now say we have a young politician

3. He later formed the Dockers & Mariners Workers Union on his return to Jamaica, the first nonpolitical trade union.

named Mike Henry who is making a lot of noise, but I know his country needs some money, so let's call him and ask him to make the coffee crop available to us for the next 10 years for a payment of $50 million. And thus we sold our patronage well in advance, for what is called selling of futures. I would have gained a great deal of credit from the public. I would have made my stars. Maybe that relates to bauxite now. I don't know.

But the point I am making is that if you analyse what I speak of in the psyche, divide and rule in the economics of the situation, you begin to fairly grasp the reality. Because, as my colleague sitting here, who is the Shadow Minister for Foreign Trade, pointed out, if the African countries begin to export beyond a certain amount of their production now, they are prevented from entering the international markets, because economics is power. That is where the power lies.

So, Mr. Speaker, I point out to the Government, there is a gap in our construction. In the Lower House I need to see a Minister of Foreign Affairs and Trade who I hope would have answered me on this point.

Mr. HENRY:

So, Mr. Speaker, through you and the Honourable House, I ask that the Minster acting on an order of Cabinet and the Prime Minister have the Ambassadors of the following countries – United Kingdom, Spain, Portugal, Netherlands, have them come into your office – and serve them with a decision of this Honourable House and seek their Governments' response to this. This is a State to a State.

Mr. Speaker, I am indeed not unmindful – and I want to make absolutely sure as I look in the gallery. I have noticed that they have not even dignified us on a debate about reparation. Not one of these embassies have dignified us with even a low-level presence in this Parliament. Mr. Speaker, perhaps after 27 years they don't believe or they believe I intend to let the matter rest with a vote. Let me, however, Mr. Speaker, show them how they could add depth and meaning to their apologies and work closely with the country to achieve real reparation. Because reparation is not cash alone, reparation is not all money that is going to help, like they say, affect the economies which are going to pay it over. This is a business. So if you owe me 200 billion and you wish to pay me over 100 years, we sit down and we negotiate that position. So all of that obfuscation doesn't impress this Member of Parliament.

I wish immediately, Mr. Speaker, on this subject, to refute from a personal perspective any arguments that they, the British, gave us an educational structure, for, Mr. Speaker, what they gave us was an elitist model meant to educate along the divide and rule concept, an educational content which carried with it content that did not reflect us or our achievements, but left us looking outside of ourselves for our solutions, and failed to impart the dignity of our African ancestry. A concept and belief, still subscribed to 'till today and manifested in the coverage and support we get from the entrenched planter class. Mr. Speaker, you cannot give me something which is my right to own.

Let's look at the debt for infrastructure and co-operative approach. And take Spain. That country's private sector is presently building large hotels. Mr. Speaker, on a government-to-government approach. Let's say Jamaica makes land available for development on a self-contained town plan, houses, schools, hospitals, health centres. The Spanish Government provides all the capital required for each development, including content and equipment. These developments are carried out in the parishes that are slated for hotels and the quality of houses pro- rated to the worker needs of the tourist industry, and the ownership of the house amortised to the workers for an agreed time, and so on. All of which is a commitment on both sides and involves a commitment which teaches self-discipline and relates to it.

Mr. Speaker, I have proposed the above as a possible approach to compensation for labour and work done in a creative element of approach, and calling on my personal experience in the world of private enterprise.

Mr. Speaker, I have referred to the Rome Treaty. On the signing of this Treaty I expect to hear from the Government. Maybe the Committee will hear. But I have not heard from the Government the reason why we haven't signed it. Do we intend to sign it? When will we sign it? What are our objections? For, Mr. Speaker, Bob Marley has been a driving force to the world. Have we failed to believe or not understand that maybe that was because he articulated the voice of the oppressed? He took us through a phase and has earned us a place in the psyche of the world. Is that the song of the century? And he did that through drawing on Garvey.

So, Mr. Speaker, I have asked myself in fighting for this motion, I have asked myself why did Gordon, Sharpe and Bogle die? Why did Sharpe, Gordon and Bogle die? Did they die that we would be sitting here bowing still to the chains that they fought against in order to make us free and not demanding from them the reparation that was due, that commitment which they fought for? Do we make them all heroes, Mr. Speaker, salute them, raise the flag and bow to 'backra master' with a 'howdy, tenk you, and we nuh bruk nuh square'. Mr. Speaker, if we continue to think like some talk-show hosts, that we do not have the power, we certainly won't have the power, and we certainly won't have it if we don't have the will.

Mr. Speaker, I am angry over the slave trade. I am angry over the slave trade and everything it has done. And if I was to return to one of the articles on slavery and what the people lived on, it would be emphasised. But, Mr. Speaker, I am equally angry when I arrive in the Cayman Islands and I see my fellow Jamaicans being treated like they were not human beings, and not people. Mr. Speaker, I am equally angry and I wonder, Mr. Speaker, do we the politicians who have failed three generations, and who should have taken it to the next level, are we once again to be the leaders of this march; once again taking our rightful place in the vanguard of Caribbean liberation politics in the true tradition of Marcus Garvey? I call on the Government and the Prime Minister, as she promised, to take the decision of this

Parliament if it is so voted, not asking them to join us. Telling them that a Private Member's Motion brought by someone who has seen the need for reparation, was passed by this House of Parliament and therefore what we are saying to them, do you want to march with us or do we leave you behind?

(Applause)

Mr. Speaker, I have often said recently, let's revolutionise the minds of our people, free them from mental slavery. Let's revolutionise the spirit of Jamaicans presently lining up at the United States Embassy, Liguanea, with no place to park, no shelter from the sun, no facility to relieve themselves **[a situation somewhat corrected]**. In answer, of course, there will be a class that says, but they do that anyway, not remembering that we didn't have a lot of these facilities when we were slaves and grew up with that expectation; a created cultural habit, Mr. Speaker. I would prefer to line up, Mr. Speaker, with the Rastafari brethren for repatriation and reparation, aiming to build a new day in Africa, than becoming a second-rate citizen in the United States. Mr. Speaker, I laud such a concept. I accept that this is where I can make it right. But if I can't make it right here, I far prefer to take that route than line up at Liguanea, waiting to have someone tell me what I can or can't do in terms of seeking an entry to somewhere else.

Let us seek this reparation for proper education through facilities at our schools. But equally important, a curriculum which speaks to us. We still have no modem history. Proper housing, proper roads, water and hospitals, leading to a revolution in production which will speak to the creative industries, so that we can write our own history and produce our own films. Let us move reggae, which we have created, to its higher forms of interpretation, and thus not let the Anglo-Saxon Protestants who so rule our psyche that we fail to grasp that we have come from the cradle of humanity, and we are entitled to our own religion and those who support their religion be allowed, not unlike the Roman Catholics, their form of celebration.

I also speak and when I speak maybe I must speak to the historical concept too. I must speak to the fact that in 1680 John Henry arrived in Trelawny, who happens to be my great, great grandfather, and was the editor of a newspaper. Maybe I must speak to the arrival of the Portugese Jews side which arrived here and lived on Jew Street in Spanish Town, among whom was the first rabbi and a Roman Catholic Archbishop sleeping in the same house. So I have no apologies to make to anyone when I speak with this aspect of my history and my time.

Mr. Speaker, a lot of what was created as racial division in slavery emanated from the Anglo-Saxon white Protestants and their claim to decendancy from the 10 lost tribes of Israel. And I say that, Mr. Speaker, because we have spoken about slavery in this context. And slavery that – slavery has always existed. And, Mr. Speaker, the house of Israel, the Anglo-Israelis out of the UK, were the ones who founded the state, and who have spoken to the coming of the house of Israel. On the other hand there is the house of Judea. Let me remind the House that Elizabeth I was the Queen who sent back all the African slaves in 1601, some 20,000 back to Africa out of England.

Mr. Speaker, I could bring the approach of the Arabs to slavery, when the words 'abede' and 'aswad' had different meanings. I could return to my roots and speak as I said. You know, I long for the day when I was going to school and they told me black was fancy, but white was corruption. It gave me a sense of some lessening of myself, but gave me a sense of the belief of the Jamaican then. But I thought, Mr. Speaker, in that context there is a racial fuss surrounding the Maoris in medieval Europe. Let me quote what I referred to.

"Muslim Maori troops from North Africa kidnapped a German navy man from the Portugese coast and forced him onto a ship. The crew is mostly light-skinned as a whole. The black African soldiers who are present among the crew members are obviously a minority. Even so, it was the exotic-looking black contingent of these armies that stirred the hearts and the imaginations of medieval Europe." So we can go back as far as we want, in terms of trying to put in context.

The older, more relative sense has been noted in other cultural areas. The Japanese once used the term 'shiroi' as white, 'kuro' as black, to describe their skin and gradations of colour. The Igbos of Nigeria were employed in the same way. So that ocho white (whiteman) and ochi black simply meant a Hebrew with a lighter complexion. In French Canada, older generations still refer to swarthy Canadians as (inaudible). Vestiges of this order and usage persist in family names. Mr. White, Mr. Brown, Mr. Black, were individuals within the normal colour spectrum. So when I speak of reparation and slavery, Mr. Speaker, I don't speak of it in racial context. As I said the racial aspect of it came from those slave traders who were given the right of the Middle Passage to move the Africans into the Caribbean, and they introduced it more racially by the fact that a lot of them were absentee runners of the estates and the plantations.

Mr. Speaker, let us not resile as a Parliament from the decision which our ancestors in their suffering, cried out for as justice. Let us hold this just reward of reparation as a touch of hope for a better future for our citizens, many of whom see very little future. For these rewards can be instantaneous, they speak to work done but not paid for. It speaks to wages for our investments made with our labour, which has grown a million-fold. It speaks to untold suffering, pain and blood flowing. It speaks to man's inhumanity and exploitation of the weak and unsuspecting for political gain, for economic gain. And it speaks to righting the injustice, the murder and the dismemberment of continents. And by all means it speaks to us not abandoning a just cause long requiring a political decision and a political commitment to seek justice in all its forms, and one that is definitely for me, not complex. It will be complex if we try to engender every single aspect of who was involved in slavery.

I speak here as the elected Member of Parliament for Central Clarendon in Jamaica. As a Private Member's Motion, I wish for a political decision by all of my colleagues to say, is reparation justified by its demand, or should we really abandon it? And we seem to be still floundering as to whether we think it is a just demand or not.

I trust the Committee, when formed, I trust that whatever comes from the amendment to the motion, I trust that what we will do from that Committee is open it up to the wider body of the country to hear of every aspect of presentation that is required.

And so, Mr. Speaker, I am aware of the co-operation of the Government by the Acting Leader of Government Business. I am aware that there are people on either side who had wished to speak to this motion. I am aware that the proposal I have is that we form a committee for this matter to be referred to, and I am aware that that Committee is hopefully going to examine and take into account all the complexities that have been made in comments. But I remain committed to one blinkered solution, perhaps it's my descendancy, perhaps it's the reality. And I am going to become very friendly to my colleague from Eastern Westmoreland, because he has already proven to us that if they stick to the case of proving that you are an ancestor of slavers, he's going to get the trillion of dollars and I want to be close to him because he is the one who is here.

So, Mr. Speaker, the motion is on the Order Paper. The amendments – I know my colleague in Central St. Catherine also suggested an amendment. I think the Committee would tie into that. I think the Leader of the Opposition spoke to the Committee examining the matter further and I think each of us want to see that further. I ask for leave of absence only in the sense that I intend to take it to the people, only in the sense of 'overstanding' it, that basically this is not a matter I have waited five years in Parliament and 20-odd years to debate and face as a person in this country. And I therefore hope that I have imbued us with the passion of commitment that just as what we read, that just as what the Leader of the Opposition read, from which showed the suffering and the pain, just as what I have spoken to and what is written in articles **let us hope that this is the forerunner of re-engineering the social structure of Jamaica. Let us hope that my other Private Member Bill which deals with Rastafari as a religion, will be addressed. Let us hope that the national registration of individuals, a Bill still lying fallow in the House, which will give the dignity of an identity to persons, will be**

readdressed. Let us hope that what we recognise is that the revolution that we require is one which makes the people recognise the responsibility of leadership, but equally the responsibility of those being led.

Let us do that within the context of letting those men who are having children, who seek to escape from one captured piece of land to the other, abandoning one woman and children for the other, are really perpetuating the slave mentality and the slave structure, and are really feeding the minds of 'backra master', rather than seeking their own sense of identity and importance. Let us not resile, Mr. Speaker, from ensuring that.

I hope that all the comments – some comments of commendation, some of criticisms – that I have heard on this matter, let me hope that what it has collectively done is awaken in the minds of the young people and the persons of Jamaica that one has to confront the realities of our past in order to build the immediacy of our future. In that context, I thank everyone for participating. I thank all my colleagues for supporting, with all the various analysis that have been raised, but let us not continue to intellectualise, and to comment on something which the reality is stark staring us in the face. This, indeed, was one of the greatest crimes against humanity within the aspect of the human lives of the Middle Passage that was created by the British, the Dutch, the French, the Spanish.

And let us be quite clear, Mr. Speaker, just as I am reminded, the Haitians who became the first free black country, paid the French for their freedom. The French willingly accepted it. The planters were paid $20 million, that is a fixed sum. All I am asking for is the same $20 million paid to Jamaica, but compounded on its growth and development over the years of slavery that we have not been paid. Whatever that comes to, pay it to the state. Let the state then elect an enlightened Government which will use it to free the minds of all of us. To let us understand there is a oneness of purpose and commitment, which is Jamaican, with the pride and dignity to lead the world. And let us in so doing, recognise that we have to be the vanguard.

And again, in closing, I say, no parliamentary body has taken a decision that is needed to drive the force of individuals who have been asking for this. I continue my search, my hope and my wish. I sincerely hope that in so speaking and speaking with the passion, that everyone will recognise – if I have said anything that would be offensive to anyone in anyway, let us just put it down to the fact that not very often in your political career you reach the point of where something you have often dreamed of is achieved by the debate. I can only hope it can be achieved by the implementation of my beliefs. Thank you very much.

(Applause)

EXTRACT FROM THE MINUTES OF THE HONOURABLE HOUSE OF REPRESENTATIVES ON THE 27th DAY OF JANUARY, 2015

PUBLIC BUSINESS

Miss Olivia Grange continued debate on the motion:

WHEREAS the economies and fortunes of Europe, including Great Britain, were largely built upon the slave trade and slave labour;

AND WHEREAS the British Parliament passed the Slavery Abolition Act, 1833, which abolished the slavery system under which the British slave owners were guaranteed an endless supply of free labour, which was critical to the productivity of their holdings;

AND WHEREAS, by further political action, the British Parliament paid to the British slave owners a sum of £20M as economic compensation for the loss of the slaves who formed a major component of their production engine;

AND WHEREAS no similar political action was taken by the British Parliament to compensate the former slaves or their descendants for their labour, which built the economies of Europe, including Great Britain, nor were the former slaves allowed to own land;

AND WHEREAS the former slaves and their descendants should have been paid for their labour, which built the economies of Europe, including Great Britain;

AND WHEREAS the Caribbean Community (CARICOM), of which Jamaica is a member, took a decision to form a committee to oversee the work of a CARICOM Reparation Commission on July 6, 2013, to pursue reparation claims against Great Britain and other slave trading countries;

AND WHEREAS the Rastafari have had their case for reparation to Africa approved by this House; and a National Reparation Committee was established by this Honourable House:

BE IT RESOLVED that this Honourable House debate the issue, as set out in the prayer, and make the political decision by a vote that the Government of Jamaica is entitled, on behalf of the former slaves and via the basic tenets of labour law and human rights, to receive payment from Great Britain, equivalent to the sum paid to the British slave owners as compensation for the loss of slave labour;

BE IT FURTHER RESOLVED that the payment be used to clear off all the debt of Jamaica and to improve the education, infrastructural development, and health sectors, and a portion be set aside for the repatriation of African Jamaicans to Africa;

AND BE IT FURTHER RESOLVED that this Honourable House enjoin other CARICOM countries to make similar political decisions on this matter, and that this Honourable House instruct the Government of Jamaica to take this case of genocide to the International Court of Justice to value the economic cost of chattel slavery to Jamaica and the further compensation that should flow for the abuse of human rights and the attendant denial of culture and history, murder, rape and wanton abuse of power in flogging, branding, and denial of freedom of movement freedom to worship, freedom to own land, and the right to education, which were the hallmark of slavery.

Miss Olivia Grange, having spoken for 30 minutes, the Minister of Science, Technology, Energy and Mining and Leader of the House moved for the suspension of the Standing Orders to enable her to continue her speech to its conclusion, notwithstanding the time limit on speeches.

Seconded by: Dr. Horace Chang.
Agreed to.

At 7:20 p.m., the Speaker interrupted. The Minister of Science, Technology, Energy and Mining and Leader of the House moved for the suspension of the Standing Orders to enable the House to sit beyond 7:30 p.m. to complete the business of the day.

Seconded by: Miss Olivia Grange.
Agreed to.

The Minister of State in the Ministry of Foreign Affairs and Foreign Trade, Honourable Arnaldo Brown; Dr. Kenneth Baugh; the Leader of the Opposition, Mr. Andrew Holness; and Mr. Pearnel Charles also spoke on the motion.

Mr. Lester Michael Henry moved that the motion be approved.
Seconded by: Mr. Rudyard Spencer.
Agreed to.

Vice Chancellor, UWI, Mona, Professor Sir Hilary Beckles, speaking on the topic 'Faked Emancipation, Insincere Independence, Reparatory Justice: A 21st Century Paradigm for Economic Growth' at a symposium held at the campus.

Cabinet Ministers Olivia 'Babsy' Grange (centre) and Mike Henry in a jovial mood alongside Dr. Kasan Troupe of the Ministry of Education at a lecture held at Denbigh High School, a major success story in May Pen, Clarendon.

Participants in a reparation baton relay exercise at Sam Sharpe Square in Montego Bay, St. James.

Hon. Mike Henry on stage on another leg of the fight for reparation.

Professor Verene Shepherd, Director of the Centre for Reparation Research, speaks out at a reparation forum.

The
Petition for Reparation

Petition to the Queen

It takes guts to stand up to the historically dominant power of our supposed motherland, Great Britain, which so cavalierly and violently exploited its colonies, including Jamaica, over centuries, and has been almost remorseless about it ever since.

History has led us to be largely subjective to the insults, the gross emotional damage, and the sheer power and might of the British, at the demise of our own well-being, destiny and overall circumstances, leaving us to be almost perpetually in the realm of a supposed 'third world' state because of our damaged egos and seemingly blighted options.

But fortunately, for at least a relatively few, there has been a central and burning focus on the raw and unquestionable realities of the sheer injustice that was for so long meted out to our ancestors from the real motherland, Africa, who were plucked from the western end of that continent and carted in amazingly dehumanising conditions to the Caribbean and Americas as chattel slaves, then worked, whipped, raped and demonised over a period of centuries to the measurable benefit of the beast of the British empire.

For that gross injustice and exploitation, the need for frontal acceptance and a commitment to seek to right the extreme wrongs has been facing the United Kingdom for so long now, and the time has finally come for real measures to be taken to realise those objectives.

This comes in the collective form of a formal petition to Her Majesty, Queen Elizabeth the Second, in concert with her Privy Council, to face and accept the reality of a reparatory claim from Jamaica, where a unanimous parliamentary vote was taken in 2015 to demand compensation from the UK for the grave injustices and debilitating negative impact of chattel slavery on Jamaica during the earlier period of British colonial occupation of the island.

None other than noted Queen's Counsel and legal luminary, Hon. Frank Phipps, OJ, QC, stepped in to lead the charge from a technical legal standpoint on Jamaica's behalf, and a petition meticulously coined under his direction, is now central to a direct demand from Great Britain for reparation for the exploitation of our ancestors during the time of chattel slavery on the island.

Frank has rallied to the cause with vigour and dexterity, to mount an impregnable position to the British Monarchy, which is to be presented with the assistance of a legal team in that country in the first direct demand from the Caribbean from the empire as a state, and the British Government as its accounting agency, to formally take responsibility for the gross misdeeds of chattel slavery, and for discussions to thereafter be held towards reaching an agreement on the forms and substantive components of reparation as a means of gradually correcting the historical sins of British-sponsored and applied chattel slavery in the region.

In the Judicial Committees of her Majesty's Privy Council

In the matter of the government of the United Kingdom of Great Britain and Ireland

And in the matter of section 4 of the Judicial Committee of the Privy Council Act 1833.

To Her Majesty in Council.

The humble Petition of the People of Jamaica presented by Lester Michael Henry, Member of Parliament of No. 1 Roosevelt Crescent, Inglewood, May Pen, in the parish of Clarendon, a Publisher and Member of the Jamaican Parliament, showeth as follows:

1. The Petition is presented under section 4 of the Judicial Committee of the Privy Council Act 1833 to Her Majesty Queen Elizabeth 11, the head of state for Jamaica and for the United Kingdom of Great Britain.

2. This Petition is presented on behalf of the overwhelming majority of the 2.7 million population ofJamaica who are the descendants of persons who had been forcibly taken from the home in Africa without their consent, and transported to Jamaica en masse, where they were sold to work on the plantations in slavery under British colonial rule until manumitted by an act of the UK government in 1838.

3. The Petitioners' ancestor were victims of crimes against humanity under British colonial rule that lasted for three hundred years from 1655 when the island of Jamaica was captured from the Spanish to the termination of colonial rule in 1962.

4. The crimes committed on the Petitioners' ancestors were perpetrated on the authority of the United Kingdom government at London until that government relinquished the authority in 1962.

5. Twelve generations of manipulation of the Petitioners' ancestors for subservience and obedience resulted in psychological damage to your Petitioners, leaving an attitude of helplessness and a culture of dependence as mental scars.

6. Jamaican financial advancement was affected by the depletion of the asset of the country for the exclusive benefit of the citizen of the UK.

7. The development of the country was left to stagnate after the enslavement was lifted.

Your Petitioner therefore humbly prays that Her Majesty will be pleased to make the following Orders:

1. "A declaration that the people of Jamaica are entitled to Reparation from the government of the United Kingdom for the crimes committed against them and their ancestors", and further

2. "An order that Reparation should be carried out as Restorative Justice where the government of the United Kingdom and representatives of the people of Jamaica address the aftermath of the offence collectively for the best interests of the country with mediator(s) appointed by the Commonwealth of Nations", and further

3. "An order for the payment of the Petitioner's costs or that such other orders may be made in the premises as to Her Majesty shall seem just".

And your Petitioner will forever pray &c.

Note: This Petition is required to be served on an authorised representative of the government of the United Kingdom.

Affidavit for Petition

◆◆◆◆◆◆

IN THE JUDICIAL COMMITTEE OF HER MAJESTY'S PRIVY COUNCIL

I Lester Michael Henry make oath and say:

1. That I am a publisher by profession and the elected member of the Jamaican House of Representative for the constituency of Central Clarendon and I reside at No. 1 Roosevelt Crescent, Inglewood, May Pen, in the parish of Clarendon.

2. I am a Minister in Government of Jamaica and I am authorized to make this affidavit for the Government of Jamaica on behalf of the people of Jamaica.

3. The overwhelming majority of Jamaica's population today are by ethnic origin, descendants of the People of Africa. The 2011 census recorded a total population of 2,684,115 million with blacks accounting for 2,471,820 million or 92.09 per cent of the total population. With the sprinkling of other ethnic groupings Jamaica is celebrated as one nation with a motto: OUT OF MANY, ONE PEOPLE. A nation of people occupying one place, all speaking one internationally recognized language. The People of Africa have lived continuously as inhabitants of the island of Jamaica; individuals and collectively, they had no other nationality or residence, or identifiable association with any other country or government other than Jamaica as a

former colony of Great Britain. The majority of the People from Africa are the only people who have inhabited the island of Jamaica continuously for more than 500 years to the present time, As the majority of the population they have elected their government under a system of universal adult franchise to administer the affairs of the country for peace, order and governance set out in the Constitution as parens patriae – the first time they had legal status to be heard in a demand for justice.

4. Jamaica was created an independent nation by the Jamaica Independence Act 1962 (UK) that states at section 3, "As from the sixth day of August, nineteen hundred and sixty-two, (in this Act referred to as 'the appointed day'), Her Majesty's Government in the United Kingdom shall have no responsibility for the government of Jamaica became a member of the United Nations," The schedule to the Act transferred legislative authority from a UK Parliament to a Jamaican Parliament without interfering with Her Majesty as the Head of State for Jamaica. Jamaica as an independent nation became a member of the United Nations on September 18, 1962.

5. The Constitution of independent Jamaica was set out in the second schedule of the Jamaica (Constitution) Order in Council 1962. The Order:

THE QUEEN'S MOST EXCELLENT MAJESTY IN COUNCIL

Her Majesty, by virtue and in exercise of the powers in that behalf by subsection (1) of section 5 of the West Indies Act 1962 or otherwise in Her vested, is pleased, by and with the advice of her Privy Council, to order, and it is hereby ordered, as follows:

(1) Subject to the provision of subsection (2) of this section and the other provisions of this Order, the Constitution of Jamaica set out in the Second Schedule to this Order (in this Order referred to as 'the Constitution') shall come into force in Jamaica at the commencement of this Order.

Chapter 1V of Schedule Two to the Order provides for a Governor-General as Her Majesty's representative in Jamaica. Chapter V provides for a Parliament, which shall consist of Her Majesty, a Senate and a House of Representatives with legislative power at section 48 to make laws for the peace, order and good governance of Jamaica. The power is circumscribed by what is stated at section 60, "A Bill shall not become law until the Governor-General has assented thereto in Her Majesty's name and on Her Majesty's behalf and has signed it in token of such assent." The Chapter VI provides Executive authority at section 68 that is vested in Her Majesty. Chapter VII establishes the Judicature with final appeal to her Majesty in Council. This constitutional arrangement confirms Her Majesty as the Head of State of Jamaica to whom the people of Jamaica have access for their protection and well-being, and for redress of the grievances to be heard ultimately by the Privy Council.

6. The Jamaican House of Representatives on the 27th of January 2015, unanimously passed a resolution moved by Hon. Mike Henry MP setting out the terms for reparation from the British Government to compensate the former slaves.

7. The Chairman of the CARICOM Prime Ministerial Sub-Committee on Reparation wrote to all heads of government

for European states that were involved in the slave trade (to the Caribbean), including the United Kingdom of Great Britain and Northern Ireland, pointing out the UN General Assembly Resolution of 23 December 2013, indicating the need for recognition, justice and development for the people of African descent, to include, "Acknowledgement and profoundly regretting the untold suffering and evils inflicted on millions of men, women and children as a result of slavery... colonialism... and past tragedies. The Resolution noted that some states have taken the initiative and it called on those who have not yet apologised and paid reparation, to find some way to contribute to the resolution of the dignity of the victims." The UK Government has not yet offered an apology and Prime Minister Cameron wrote in response to letter dated 22 April 2016, saying, Foreign Secretary Hague "made it clear that the British Government does not believe that reparation are the answer."

8. Thomas Clarkson reports: The first importation of slaves from Africa, by our countrymen, was in the reign of Elizabeth, in the year 1562. The Queen was greatly concerned about these events: She (Elizabeth 1), seems to have been aware of the evils to which its continuance might lead, ot that, if it were sanctioned, the most unjustifiable means might be made use of to procure the persons of the natives of Africa. Summoning Captain John Hawkins, to brief her regarding his voyage to Africa, the Queen: expressed her concern lest any of the Africans should be carried off without their free consent, declaring that "it would be detestable, and call down the vengeance of heaven upon the undertakers."

9. Despite the Queen's injunction, the transporting of People from Africa to Jamaica by the British continued to 1808 when the Parliament of the United Kingdom passed the Abolition of the Slave Trade Act 1807, thereby acknowledging responsibility to restrict the horrid practice in which they were involved. Slavery remained legally acceptable in Jamaica and most of the British Empire until the Parliament of the United Kingdom in further acknowledgement of accountability, terminated the evil by the Slave Abolition Act 1833 that became fully effective in Jamaica in 1838.

10. During that period, men, women and children were seized from different parts of Africa and transported against their will for sale to settlers to work on plantations in enslavement – deprived of their humanity like any other piece of machinery of the agricultural industry owned and operated by the planters. The estimated 1.5 million who arrived in Jamaica were dispersed to plantations throughout the island in enslavement; undiscriminating on origin, status, culture and language – as strangers to each other, to work for the economic benefit of the planters in Jamaica and at home in Britain. Their enslavement under British rule lasted for 183 years, working without compensation or compassion, and without hope of relief from their misery until death or manumission by an Act of the UK Parliament. This was at a time when English law did not allow Slavery on English soil as was confirmed in Somerset's Case in 1772. A period celebrated by some as the time of Britain's greatest prosperity, a period bemoaned by many as the time of humankind's greatest tragedy.

11. Chattel Slavery with unimaginable abuse started with the seizure of people from different parts of Africa, forcibly carrying them in mass from their homes to the West Coast of Africa and transporting them across an ocean in inhumane conditions to Jamaica for sale. Their enslavement in Jamaica with severe deprivation of physical and mental freedom, working in cruel and brutal conditions on the plantations without compensation or the hope of relief for 183 years was the appalling history of life of the chattel slave in Jamaica under British rule.

12. The enslaved in Jamaica and elsewhere in the Caribbean lived in an atmosphere of oppression. Capital and other forms of punishment (eg. imprisonment, dismemberment) were meted out for acts such as striking a white person, running away, burning cane fields or theft. For some acts or resistance deemed 'offensive', they were branded with hot irons, had their noses split or, in the case of men, (were) even castrated.

13. Thomas Thistlewood from Lincolnshire, England, a particularly cruel enslaver, devised various cruel punishments for the

enslaved. One of his infamous acts was 'Derby's Dose', according to which he forced one enslaved man to defecate into the mouth of another, and then gagged him (the receiver) for four or five hours. Thistlewood would also whip enslaved Africans, rub "salt pickle, lime juice and bird pepper" in the open wounds, as well as force enslaved men to urinate in the eyes and mouths of others. He sometimes rubbed molasses all over the enslaved, then left them naked outside overnight to be devoured by mosquitos.

16. Wars of Resistance were frequent occurrences in slave societies. Enslavement with the cruelties inflicted on the People did not go unchallenged. The first recorded resistance to slavery (in Jamaica) was the Revolt at Sutton Plantation in 1690 that was followed by several (other) revolts and rebellions island-wide: Outstanding were two in Trelawny at the west – the Maroon wars, the Chief Tacky rebellion at the centre, and Queen Nanny of the Maroons at the east. Finally, the Sam Sharpe resistance (the Christmas Rebellion/Sam Sharpe War) 1831-1832, one year before the Emancipation Act. Enslaved Africans would be executed for participating in the armed struggle. In the case of the Sam Sharpe War, rebel leaders were executed in public ceremonies. Many were flogged ten to five hundred times, however, most were hanged, shot or decapitated.

17. The complaint in the Petition concerns the denial of humanity for people in Jamaica under British rule, disallowing them the protection of law for the fundamental rights and freedoms of the individual – carried out, condoned and facilitated by successive governments of the United Kingdom without remorse or apology, or an offer of redress now long overdue to heal the pain of post-trauma stress.

18. The Slavery Abolition Act of 1833 did not only abolish slavery; perversely, the emphasis in the legislature was compensation for loss of property by the slave owners, but nothing for the enslaved People who had lost more by their enslavement. The loss of their humanity and basic rights during the entire period of their enslavement under British rule went unrequited up to the time of independence in 1962.

The insufferable hardship and misery continued, if not worsened, when discarded from plantations - dispossessed of property to wander penniless, unskilled and uneducated in a land where they lived for 344 years without knowing a way back home, and without knowing any other home.

19. The abolition of slavery did not end British terrorism against the people of Jamaica. The post-slavery period was called the period of racial apartheid, and was marked by broken promises to indentured labourers from India, racism, 'classism/castism' and a myriad of injustices against freed Africans who protested continuing British brutality. Resistance against injustices was met with extreme forms of punishment, for example, the execution of Paul Bogle and the hundreds of those he led in the Morant Bay war in 1865.

20. Protests against poor labour conditions were met with police brutality in the 1930s. Collective bargaining and representation through trade unions were discouraged; so was the right to vote by all adults regardless of ethnicity. Today, Jamaica is independent: but the scars of British colonialism linger. There was no financial independence settlement, no 'Marshall Plan' to assist the new nation to deal with the problems that would beset it in independence. Despite the best efforts of the island's people, the social and physical infrastructure are well below par. Classism, racism, structural discrimination, distance from an African identity and other social ills refuse to go away. So intense was British attempt to make Africans feel inferior to Europeans.

21. A reparatory justice package is still due!! Sir Ellis Clarke, who was the Trinidadian Government's UN representative to a sub-committee of the Committee on Colonialism in 1964, made this point in his statement: "An administering power... is not entitled to extract for centuries all than can be got out of a colony and when that has been done, to relieve itself of its obligations by the conferment of a formal but meaningless – meaningless because it cannot possibly be supported – political independence. Justice requires that reparation be made to the country that has suffered the ravages of colonialism before that country is expected to face up to the problems and difficulties that will inevitably

beset it upon independence." Europe's alternative strategy of grants and ODA is not the answer. Reparatory and de-colonial justice is. Reparation payment allocated appropriately will likely have economically positive and statistically significant impacts on growth and development.

22. A first generation consideration of the issues for reparation must recognize that Her Majesty is the Head of State of Jamaica and all the people in Jamaica enjoy Her Majesty's protection; unlawful and unjust treatment of the People is remediable at the instance of Her Majesty's Government in Her Majesty's courts in Jamaica. Her Majesty is also the Head of State of the United Kingdom of Great Britain and Northern Ireland where the servants and agents of the Government act in Her Majesty's name. The former affords protection, the latter demands accountability.

23. The answer to the question whether the people of Jamaica have access to Her Majesty for redress for the wrongs committed against their ancestors during the period of British rule in Jamaica is provided by the authority of section 4 of the Judicial Committee of the Privy Council 1833 that provides, "It shall be lawful for His Majesty to refer to the said judicial committee for hearing or consideration any such other matters whatsoever as His Majesty shall think fit." The practice is to advise Her Majesty to refer to the Judicial Committee under this Section only cases of constitutional importance in which an advisory opinion is required by the Government or this House on a point which cannot be effectively decided in the ordinary courts. Section 4 is also the section for access to Her Majesty for removal of a judge for misbehavior.

24. The Charter establishing the International Military Tribunal in Nuremberg in 1945 after World War 11, for the first time defined the prosecuted crimes against humanity. The Rome Statute of the International Criminal Court Article 7 provides: Crimes against humanity 1. For the purpose of this Statute, 'crime against humanity' means any of the following acts when committed as part of a widespread or systematic attack directed against any civilian population, with knowledge of the attack: (a) Murder; (b) Extermination (c) Enslavement

(d) Deportation or forcible transfer of population; (e) Imprisonment or other severe deprivation of physical liberty in violation of fundamental rules of international law. The UN Convention on Statutory Limitations to Crimes Against Humanity states the Convention on the Non-Applicability of Statutory Limitations to War Crimes and Crimes Against Humanity Article 1 (b) Crimes against humanity whether committed in time of war or in time of peace as they are defined in the Charter of the International Military Tribunal, Nuremberg, of August 1945 and confirmed by resolution 3 (1) of 13 February 1946 and 95 (i) of 11 December 1946 of the General Assembly of the United Nations.

25. The fact that the complaint relates to activities that took place before slavery was abolished 180 years ago, since then, not only time has moved on, a sense of justice with the commonality of human rights has evolved to prevail over the dictates of time that would impose limits on accountability for crimes against humanity.

26. The laws passed and enforced by the House of Assembly for slavery were repugnant to the Laws of England and contrary to the authority set out in the Royal Commission to Lord Windsor in 1662. The Royal Commission to Lord Windsor empowered him to govern the island in accordance with "all such reasonable laws, customs and institutions as are exercised and settled in our other colonies and plantations, or such others as shall upon mature advice and consideration be held necessary and proper for the good government of Jamaica and the said Islands adjacent to Jamaica, provided that they be not repugnant to our laws of England, but agreeing thereto as near as the conditions or affairs will permit."

27. The unpaid work, the denial of due process of law and the cruel and inhumane abuse of human rights are all wrongs in which the UK Government was complicit. The answer to this question is finally put beyond doubt by the Preamble to the Act of Parliament 23 Geo 11 Cap.31: "Whereas the trade to and from Africa is very advantageous to Great Britain, and necessary for the supplying (of) the plantations, and colonies thereunto belonging, with a sufficient number of negroes, at reasonable rates."

Deceit and the Fight for Resolution

In terms of the realities that now face Britain relative to the imminence of reparatory justice for Jamaica and the wider Caribbean for the grave injustices of the slave era, some stark facts have and are emerging on the global stage.

For example, on September 20, 2015 when then British Prime Minister, David Cameron, addressed the Jamaican Parliament during his visit to the island, he told Jamaica and the region that slavery was a long time ago and it was time black people 'get over it'.

But the reality of that moment was nothing short of extraordinary, as it has since emerged that while Cameron spoke, Britain had just finished paying off the slavery abolition loan of 1834.

Historians have now gotten to the bottom of that colossal falsehood with the subsequent revelation that Britain paid the last installment of the 1834 slavery abolition loan on February 15, 2015. That revelation spoke most potently of the falsehood of the British position that slavery was such a distant event that it should be viewed as of remote historical significance with no connection or relevance to the present time.

The Centre for Reparatory Research put paid to that notion at a press conference at the University of the West Indies (UWI) Regional Headquarters, Mona, Jamaica, on February 21, 2018. There it was revealed that the persistent dishonesty on the matter by British governments and prime ministers had been exposed by evidence from Her Majesty's Treasury, which showed that the slavery loan was refinanced several times and finally paid off only three years earlier. So much for being irrelevant and a distant memory!

At the press conference, Vice-Chancellor of the The University of the West Indies (The UWI), Professor, Sir Hilary Beckles, who is also an economic historian, revealed that research into the archives of the Bank of England, Her Majesty's Treasury, and Rothchild Merchant Bank, showed that successive recent British prime ministers, especially Tony Blair and David Cameron, sought to deceive the Caribbean people on the matter of the region's claim for reparation.

The press conference was told that while British political leaders have refused to enter into reparation conversation with the Caribbean on the basis that slavery was in the distant past and hence not subject to reparation claims, the British government had refinanced the slave loan for over 150 years in order to benefit from slavery, right under the nose of the Caribbean people.

In describing the deception as being shameful and disgraceful, the Caribbean Reparation Commission said it was "unimaginable that until 2015 ordinary people in Britain, including blacks, were still repaying the slave abolition loan which equates to over £20 billion in today's money."

The commission noted that in addition to a general apology on the horrors of the slave system and discussions towards a settlement on reparation for the Caribbean region, the British government needs to apologise for the gross deception of the Caribbean people up to the present time.

But with conscience of some sort emerging out of the United Kingdom, just over a year ago, Glasgow University announced that it was owning up to having benefited from wealth that was accrued on the back of the British slave system, and would be making reparation in recognition of that fact.

In September 2018, the university announced that it is making reparation after admitting that it had made £200 million from the transatlantic slave trade.

A report on the matter in the Guardian.com cited Sir Geoff Palmer, Scotland's first black professor, as welcoming the ground-breaking report into how Glasgow University benefited from the procurement of slavery. Professor Palmer is reported to have said the development posed "uncomfortable questions" for the British society as a whole, and called on institutions that similarly profited from the slave trade to make amends.

Of note is that Glasgow University was at the forefront of the 19th century movement to abolish slavery. It will now create a centre for the study of slavery and a memorial or tribute in the name of the enslaved, and is also reportedly working to establish ties with the University of the West Indies.

Palmer, professor emeritus at the school of life sciences at Heriot-Watt University in Edinburgh, UK, spoke clearly and glaringly on the lessons and implications of the Glasgow report.

"Now I think the country faces a very uncomfortable question which the Glasgow University report has raised once more: to what extent did slavery make Scotland great?" he asked.

While paying tribute to the Glasgow report and the university's desire to make reparation, he put both Scotland and the UK overall on notice.

"We can have all the equality laws and anti-racism legislation we like," he said, "but if no other institutions, firms or organisations which also benefitted from slavery declare this and seek to make amends, then it is all meaningless.

"If they all were to follow the example of Glasgow University, then that would be real race relations... if what Glasgow University is doing in reaching out to these communities as a means of reparation were to be replicated, it would make a difference."

The media report cited the "evils of slavery" as having been "stitched into the very fabric of Glasgow for almost 200 years, with a district, Merchant City, having been built on the tobacco trade which profited from appallingly inhumane acts during slavery, and a number of prominent streets in the city overall, were named after "some of the most notorious exploiters of the slave market, while Jamaica, Tobago and Virginia are similarly commemorated."

News Release

£20 million University of Glasgow reparation agreement with The UWI

For release upon receipt - AUGUST 2, 2019

UWI

The University of the West Indies (The UWI) and the University of Glasgow have signed the first ever agreement for slavery reparation since British Emancipation in 1838.

The £20 million agreement was signed at the Regional Headquarters of The UWI in Kingston, Jamaica on July 31, 2019 by Vice-Chancellor, Professor Sir Hilary Beckles, and Dr David Duncan, University of Glasgow's Chief Operating Officer, representing Vice-Chancellor, Professor Sir Anton Muscatelli.

The terms of the agreement call for the University of Glasgow to provide £20 million to fund research to promote development initiatives to be jointly undertaken with The UWI over the next two decades. The sum of £20 million was the amount paid to slave owners as reparation by the British government when it abolished slavery in 1834.

The agreement represents the first occasion on which a slavery-enriched British or European institution has apologised for its part in slavery and committed funds to facilitate a reparation programme. In this instance, the two universities have adopted a regional development approach to reparation.

The funds will facilitate the operations of a jointly-owned and managed institution to be called the Glasgow-Caribbean Centre for Development Research. The Centre will target and promote solutions to Caribbean development problems in areas such as medicine and public health, economics and economic growth, cultural identity and cultural industries, and other 21st century orientations in Caribbean transformation.

The seminal agreement, the first of its kind in the Western World, brings to closure negotiations between the two institutions that began when the University of Glasgow published a report in 2018 revealing that between the 1780s and 1880s, it received millions of pounds in grants and endowments from Scottish and English slave owners that served to enrich and physically expand the near 600-year-old university.

Professor Sir Hilary Beckles, who brokered the historic agreement, commended Dr Duncan for his astute leadership of the Glasgow Reparatory Justice Task Force, and Glasgow's Vice-Chancellor, Professor Sir Anton Muscatelli, for his visionary leadership.

Commenting on the globally anticipated moment in the long reparation struggle, Sir Hilary noted that the University of Glasgow acknowledged that a university cannot be excellent if it is not ethical, and that the agreement places the university on a high moral ground.

The £20 million will be invested in policy research in science, technology, society and economy, and education and advocacy that seek to repair the debilitating consequences of slavery and colonisation that continue to hold back Caribbean development. The centre will therefore focus on joint efforts to clean up the colonial mess that continues to subvert efforts at Caribbean social growth and economic growth. It will be formally established on the two campuses in September 2019.

About the University of Glasgow

Founded in 1451, the University of Glasgow is the fourth oldest university in the English-speaking world, delivering world-class, world-changing research and education with impact. A member of the prestigious Russell Group of leading UK universities, Glasgow is ranked 67th in the world (QS World University Rankings 2020) and joint 93rd in the world by the Times Higher Education World University Rankings 2019. It welcomes students from more than 140 countries worldwide and have around 28,000 undergraduate and postgraduate students.

About The UWI

For over 70 years, The University of the West Indies (The UWI) has provided service and leadership to the Caribbean region and wider world. The UWI has evolved from a university college of London in Jamaica with 33 medical students in 1948, to an internationally respected, regional university with near 50,000 students and four campuses: Mona in Jamaica, St. Augustine in Trinidad and Tobago, Cave Hill in Barbados, and an Open Campus. As part of its robust globalisation agenda, The UWI has established partnering centres with universities in North America, Latin America, Asia, and Africa, including the State University of New York (SUNY)-UWI Center for Leadership and Sustainable Development; the Canada-Caribbean Studies Institute with Brock University; the Strategic Alliance for Hemispheric Development with Universidad de los Andes (UNIANDES); the UWI-China Institute of Information Technology, the University of Lagos (UNILAG)-UWI Institute of African and Diaspora Studies, and the Institute for Global African Affairs with the University of Johannesburg (UJ).

The UWI offers over 800 certificate, diploma, under-graduate and postgraduate degree options in Food & Agriculture, Engineering, Humanities & Education, Law, Medical Sciences, Science & Technology, Social Sciences and Sport.

As the region's premier research academy, The UWI's foremost objective is driving the growth and development of the regional economy. *Times Higher Education* ranked The UWI among the top 1,258 universities in the world for 2019, and the 40 best universities in its Latin America Rankings for 2018. The UWI was the only Caribbean-based university to make the prestigious lists.

Perhaps equally notable from a British perspective was the November 2018 admission from Prince Charles, heir to the British Throne, that Britain's involvement in the transatlantic slave trade was an appalling atrocity that has left an "indelible stain" on the world.

The British standard bearer made the comments in a speech in Ghana, from where many Africans were shipped away to a life of slavery, most across the Atlantic, on ships from Britain and other nations, the Guardian reported.

Charles said virtually the opposite of what David Cameron said in Jamaica in 2015.

In noting that the "profound injustice" of the legacy of the slave trade and slavery could never be forgotten, Charles elaborated that: "At Osu Castle on Saturday, it was especially important to me, as indeed it was on my first visit there 41 years ago, that I should acknowledge the most painful chapter of Ghana's relations with the nations of Europe, including the United Kingdom.

"The appalling atrocity of the slave trade, and the unimaginable suffering it caused, left an indelible stain on the history of our world."

The Guardian said Charles visited Christiansborg Castle in Osu, which originally operated as a Danish slave trade fort, and from where it is estimated that more than 1.5 million Africans were forced into slavery.

In further contrasting Cameron's statement, Charles said: "While Britain can be proud that it later led the way in the abolition of this shameful trade, we have a shared responsibility to ensure that the abject horror of slavery is never forgotten," he told his audience in Ghana.

Of very significant note is that the Caribbean Community (CARICOM) in general has formulated a 10-point action plan towards truth, justice and reconciliation as the basis for negotiation with Denmark, France, Spain, The Netherlands, the United Kingdom and other European States for reparatory justice. This action plan is comprised of the following:

1. A full and formal apology accepting responsibility, committing to non-repetition and pledging to repair the harm that has been caused by the slave system. Statements of regret only are not good enough.

2. Indigenous people development programmes, with the former colonising European States taking on responsibility to support these programmes.

3. Funding for repatriation and resettlement of persons desirous of returning to Africa, including the issues of citizenship and re-integration.

4. The establishment of cultural institutions and the return of cultural heritage to right the wrongs of systematic destruction of the cultural identities and language of the indigenous people, the enslaved Africans, and the indentured workers.

5. Addressing and remedying the public health crisis in the Caribbean through the injection of more modern science, technology and capital generally into the systems within the region.

6. Education programmes to bolster the efforts of the Caribbean region to catch up with the world, having inherited a flawed and inadequate system built on structural discrimination, which has hampered the drive for social and economic development regionally.

7. The enhancement of historical and cultural knowledge exchanges to help correct centuries of disconnection and restore greater pride among the people of the Caribbean region and rebuild 'bridges of belong'.

8. Psychological rehabilitation after the inter-generational transmission of trauma. The history of colonialism by European States has generally inflicted serious psychological trauma on indigenous and African descendant people, who now need rehabilitation for their affected population, including mental health issues and some other manifestations of illness.

9. The right to development through the use of technology. For centuries, the trade and production of Europe could be summed up in the British slogan: "Not a nail is to be made in the colonies". That was a deliberate decision to retard the technology available for development with Caribbean states. Technology transfer and science sharing for development is

therefore an important part of repairing the deliberate harm to the development prospects of Caribbean countries.

10. Debt cancellation and monetary compensation. Caribbean countries which emerged from slavery have inherited the massive crisis of community poverty and inability to adequately deal with the development of the respective countries because of the burdens of the legacy of colonialism. In the efforts to overcome those challenges, such states have racked up onerous levels of debt, which rightly belong to a great extent to the colonial states which made no meaningful attempt to deal with the debilitating legacy of colonialism. Support for the payment of domestic debt, the cancellation of international debt, and direct monetary payments, where appropriate, are necessary reparatory actions to genuinely correct the harm caused by colonialism.

Hon. Michael Henry (right), presents a copy of his publication, 'Many Rivers to Cross – A Political Journey of Audacious Hope', to Reparation Activist, Esther Stanford, when she visited him at Jamaica House in May 2019.

Dub poet and talk-show host, Mutabaruka (second left); First daughter of Kwame Nkrumah, the first President of Ghana, Samia Yaba Christina Nkrumah (second left); and son of National Hero, Marcus Garvey, Dr Julius Garvey (fourth left), unveil a plaque at the official launch of the University of the West Indies, Mona's Centre for Reparation on October 10, 2017. Sharing in the moment are (from left) Vice-Chancellor, UWI Mona and Chair, CARICOM Reparation Commission, Professor Sir Hilary Beckles, and Director, Centre for Reparation Research, Professor Verene Shepherd.

Steven Golding, President of the Universal Negro Improvement Association (UNIA), addresses a function on reparation. Prominent within the audience is noted constitutional lawyer, Frank Phipps QC (right foreground).

Culture Minister, Olivia 'Babsy' Grange (left), cheering on youth participants at a reparation function.

Memories of the Fight

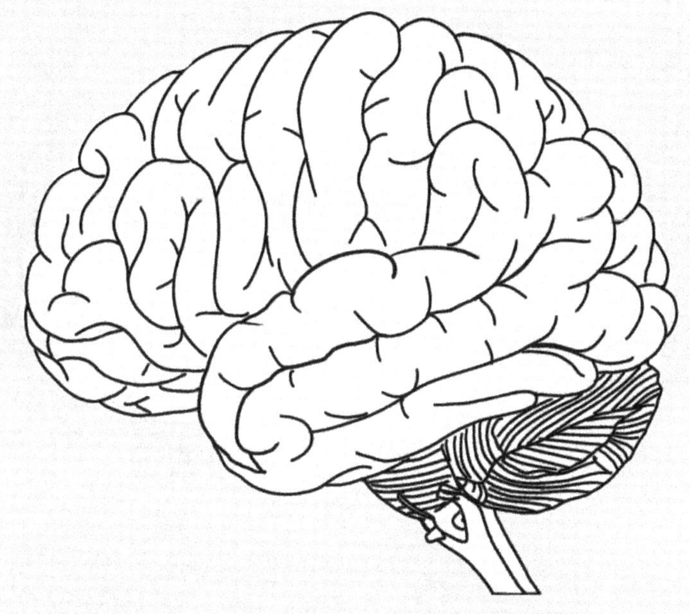

Articles from The Jamaica Observer and The Gleaner Company

Speech from Jamaica Stock Exchange Conference

(2007 - 2014)

The subject of reparation has been consistently on the global stage over the last few decades, and not to be outdone, the question of European responsibility for the atrocities of chattel slavery in the Caribbean centuries ago, has also been on the regional and local media landscapes.

From opinion pieces to news reports and other developments amid debate on the issue, it has all been there.

Here in Jamaica, from the dialogue and debate on my private member's motion in Parliament, to the work of the national and regional commissions on reparation, the 2015 visit of then British Prime Minister David Cameron, and reparatory developments in both Europe and the United States of America, the media has stoutly kept the nation abreast of the fight for reparation.

From that broad mass of local media output on the subject, a few of the local pieces were selected for direct mention. These, primarily from the nation's top newspapers, The Gleaner Company and the Jamaica Observer, have certainly helped to keep the population up to date on the drive towards reparation and the broad national benefits to be accrued from success in this endeavour.

A sincere gratitude is being extended to the local media, including the national newspapers, for their inputs, and it is hoped and anticipated that their support will continue in this regard.

Among the Jamaican media coverage of reparations over the years has been reportage of the parliamentary engagements on the subject over the period, including in December 2012 when House member, Mike Henry, slammed then House Speaker, Michael Peart, for reportedly failing to stick to a schedule for the start of the debate on Henry's private member's motion on reparations.

Fuming over the delay, Henry cited disrespect after being told that the House would instead be going on recess, this although he claimed that the debate had been scheduled and the Government had given a commitment to have a conscience vote on the matter after the deliberations in Parliament, yet the unplanned delay had arisen.

Henry expressed disappointment about the development, which he said was similarly disappointing to many other Jamaicans.

Likewise, the same year, Henry had occasion, as was reported in the local media, to lambast then Prime Minister, Portia Simpson Miller, after Simpson Miller reportedly stated on behalf of Jamaica, that the country would not be seeking reparation for slavery from Britain.

"I am very saddened that in this our 50th anniversary (as a country), because of the visit of a Prince Harry..., the prime minister has taken this stance," said Henry in a media interview then.

In describing Simpson Miller's assertion as having been misguided and not in concert with the outcome of public consultations on the matter, Henry declared that "The prime minister cannot speak for me on my private member's motion. She should not seek to preempt a vote that I am asking for."

Eight years later, it is clear how that 'fight' went.

Timeline: 2007

February 16, 2007

Jamaican MP Calls for Reparations for Slavery

By Edmond Campbell,
Senior News Coordinator

The historic debate on reparations for people of African ancestry began in the House of Representatives last week with the mover of the motion, Member of Parliament for Central Clarendon, Mike Henry making an impassioned plea for Parliament to send an unequivocal message to the then slave-trading nations that the time had come for reparations to be made to those who were brutally enslaved.

With a fervor befitting the subject matter that was being debated, Mr. henry declared that he felt very strongly about the issue, and his passion carried with it "no less a revolutionary zeal than when I was a teen".

The motion addresses specific matters as it relates to reparation.

It called on the House to establish a united and common position on the proposition that reparation was due to the countries of the displaced descendants.

Further, it pushes for the establishment of a committee of the House to quantify the reparation. And, the motion wants nations due to make reparation to be called upon to provide compensation by way to cash and or debt relief.

Mr. Henry, who is also a publisher, said he had conducted extensive research on the subject, and had not found one case where a sovereign Parliament "who has suffered from slavery" had voted on the entitlement of reparations "and I demand from my Parliament such a decision, a decision which if made by a government would I feel sanction the pursuance of this matter to the highest world court; and have that world court reject this justified plea or accept it."

In acknowledgement that in recent times heads of states,

monarchs and presidents have tendered apologies for slavery, Mr. Henry said he was not averse to accepting apologies which by their very issuance carried with it guilt and responsibility.

However, he said that was not good enough as apologies should be accompanied by compensation equal to the act.

During his presentation, Mr. Henry quoted extensively from magazines and papers to support his argument for reparation.

He said if the British, the French, the Dutch and Portuguese were not willing to have dialogue and take responsibility for their involvement in slavery, and approach a settlement in real economic terms, similar to how they settled with the slave owners, parliamentarians should seek reparations in the highest courts of justice.

"So whether reparations come in the form of payments tied to infrastructure of education, I ask that we as a Parliament decide what we feel is just; let us clearly stake out our position on slavery and its impact on our lives," he asserted.

Painting a graphic picture of the multiple acts of barbarism during slavery, Mr. Henry pointed to murder, enslavement, deportation, torture and rape.

He reminded his colleagues that reparations have been paid for harm inflicted on the Jews, pointing out that since World War II, Germany had paid at least $88 billion Deutsche Marks in reparations to the State of Israel and had made another $20 billion disbursement to the same nation in 2005.

300,000 murdered

Mr. Henry argued that the Chinese were discussing the possibility of suing the Government of Japan for the atrocities committed during the capture of the city of Nangking, which resulted in the systematic murder of more than 300,000 Chinese by Japanese soldiers during World War II.

So-called comfort women from Korea who were forced into prostitution during World War II by the Japanese have also planned to sue the Japanese government for reparations.

Member of Parliament for Kingston Central, Victor Cummings, who also participated in the debate, said the teaching of African history and civilisation in schools, would help to break the bonds of mental slavery.

"We need to get rid of mental slavery as a lot of what is happening within our country has to do with that mental slavery. We find it hard to work together as a people because it is entrenched in our psyche from long ago," he stated. He argued that the passage of the resolution by itself would not go far enough in achieving what was necessary for the country at this time.

"Just passing a resolution alone even if you have full support, will not go far in achieving what needs to be achieved. We need to be out in the schools and us as leaders of our country need to lead by example," he contended.

Timeline: 2012

April 19, 2012

Parliament Not Ready to Take Vote on Reparation - Hanna

By Daraine Luton,
Senior Staff Reporter

MINISTER OF Youth and Culture Lisa Hanna on Tuesday proposed that any parliamentary deliberation of reparation from Britain be delayed.

Hanna told the House of Representatives that a Reparations Commission, which was set up to do national consultations, has not met since February 2010, because it has no money to conduct its work.

"This honourable House will not be in a position to make the kind of decisions being recommended, including taking the necessary vote, without the report of the consultation with the wider constituency of the Jamaican citizenry, as well as the information that we will need from the Reparations Committee," Hanna said.

Britain should pay

Central Clarendon Member of Parliament Mike Henry, in opening the debate to a private member's motion he brought to the House, said Britain should pay with "cold, hard cash as debt relief".

"Great Britain, of all the slave countries, paid the Caribbean slave owners of the Caribbean compensation for losing their chattels and human animals and they have not yet paid the slaves," Henry said.

Stressing the need for the Parliament to vote on the matter, Henry said, "a decision which is made by a government would sanction the pursuance of the matter to the highest world court and have the world court reject or accept the position.

"I feel we have resiled from the political decisions," he said. "We have allowed the lead to be taken by individuals and organisation of legal minds," he added.

But Hanna said the House will need to be guided by the report of a Commission of Reparation that was set up to undertake, among other things, public consultations.

Hanna told the House that former Culture Minister Olivia 'Babsy' Grange had set up a Reparations Committee in May 2009 to do groundwork on the issue.

She, however, said the commission's work ceased in February 2010 due to financial limitations.

"By June 2010, CHASE was approached on the recommendation of the Cabinet to provide funding for the continuation of the commission's work, estimated then at $26 million and reduced for submission to CHASE to $14 million," Hanna said.

She added: "CHASE was not able to accede to the request for the assistance."

Motion suspended

Following the intervention of the minister, the debate on the motion was suspended until next Tuesday.

In March, Prime Minister Portia Simpson Miller said her administration would not be seeking reparation from Britain.

"I have heard the calls, I am not making any call on the British government about whether they pay or give us compensation," the prime minister said.

Simpson Miller said slavery was "wicked, it was brutal", arguing that "No race should have been subjected to what our ancestors were subjected to."

Nonetheless, she indicated that her Government would accept an apology from Britain for the atrocities.

"We gained our freedom on the sweat, blood and tears of our ancestors and we are now free. If Britain wishes to apologise, fine with us, no problem at all," she said.

Henry said an apology would not suffice.

"I have no problem with receiving or accepting apologies, which by their very essence and their issuance carry a guilt and a responsibility. That is not good enough, it must carry with it compensation to the act," Henry said.

May 9, 2012

Mike Henry to Boycott Parliament over Reparations

Member of Parliament for Central Clarendon, Mike Henry, says he will be staying away from the opening of Parliament tomorrow to protest what he says was the snubbing of his private member's motion on reparations.

Last Tuesday, leader of government business, Phillip Paulwell, told Parliament that a vote would not be taken on the motion as an MP who was not present at the sitting wanted to make a contribution to the debate.

Henry insisted the motion was too important for the vote to be delayed to accommodate just one person.

However, the sitting was later adjourned without the vote.

Henry says it is disappointing that in the country's 50th year of Independence from Great Britain, an important issue such as reparations is being treated with scant regard by the leader of government business.

He says he considers the decision not to take the vote before Parliament prorogued the greatest insult to our African ancestry.

Timeline: 2013

January 30, 2013

Even 'On a Stretcher', Henry Vows to Continue Reparations Fight

By Daraine Luton,
Senior Staff Reporter

Three Government members yesterday joined forces with Central Clarendon Member of Parliament Mike Henry in voting against an amendment to a motion on reparations.

The amendment, which was passed, served as a fly in the ointment for Henry, who was seeking to have the House appoint a committee to sit jointly with members of the Senate to discuss in consultation with private and/or governmental bodies the issue of reparations from Britain directly or, if necessary, through the highest international courts.

Government Members of Parliament Paul Buchanan, Julian Robinson and Jolyan Silvera, as well as Henry and his Opposition colleague Rudyard Spencer, voted 'no' to the amendment which was moved by Leader of Government Business, Phillip Paulwell.

Paulwell said owing to the fact that the National Commission on Reparations for Slavery, which was launched in May 2009, was reconvened in 2012 and is actively involved in research, the motion should be deferred until the commission reports its findings.

Matter of Urgency

"The proposed amendment is not in any way to deny and to vote negatively against this issue of reparation, but is to recognise that there is a process in place started by the former regime," Paulwell said.

He added: "We are going to ensure and insist that it be expedited so that this Parliament gets a report as a matter of urgency."

Henry insisted that the amendment be put to a vote.

When Clerk of the Houses of Parliament Heather Cooke took the names, 26 persons voted 'yes', five persons voted 'no' and six declined to vote.

Those who abstained were Dr. Dayton Campbell, Pearnel Charles, Olivia Grange, Gregory Mair, Desmond McKenzie and Lloyd B. Smith.

Twenty-five members were absent for the vote, among them Dr. Ken Baugh, who walked out while Cooke was conducting the exercise.

The fight for reparations has been championed for years by Henry. He noted that it has been the case that the Parliament has not dealt with the matter, but signalled that he would not stop fighting.

"Some people may want to see me go, I will bring it back next year... Suspend it and by the resuscitation, I am coming back on a stretcher to bring it back again," Henry declared.

Timeline: 2014

September 22, 2014

House to Resume Reparations Debate

By Balford Henry,

Senior Staff Reporter

KINGSTON, Jamaica – The House of Representatives is to resume debate on the motion from Member of Parliament for Central Clarendon, Mike Henry, seeking reparations from Britain for Jamaicans who are descendants of the victims of the African slave trade.

This was indicated by Leader of the House of Representatives, Phillip Paulwell, as he sought approval last Tuesday for the debate's suspension until the next session of Parliament, which begins on Thursday.

It is expected that Minister of Youth and Culture, Lisa Hanna, will table the report of the revived Reparations Commission, chaired by Professor Verene Shepherd, which has already been approved by the Cabinet, when it resumes.

A reparations commission appointed by former minister of culture, Olivia 'Babsy' Grange, was chaired by Professor Barry Chevannes until his death in November 2010. He was replaced by Professor Shepherd, when it was reconvened by Hanna in 2012. However, the work of the commission continued to be hampered by a lack of resources.

Opening the debate, Henry appealed to his colleagues in the House to make the political decision he says is required to ensure that it is taken as far as the international court of Justice (ICJ).

"I am asking the government, as we await the reparations report, to support this effort on behalf of the younger generation. We need to balance the issues and really move the country forward, "the opposition MP said.

His Private Member's Motion, which has been the subject of discussions in the House for more than three years, asks

Parliament to establish "a united and common position and take a vote acknowledging that reparation is due to the countries of the displaced descendants of the African peoples, and that the Government of Jamaica has the right to pursue such claims from Great Britain on behalf of all citizens of Jamaica."

Henry told the Observer that he welcomed CARICOM's decision to make the issue a regional one, and added that he had no problem with Prime Minister Portia Simpson Miller's request that a "non-confrontational" approach be taken.

A number of prominent Rastafarians, including singer Bunny Wailer, attended the sitting at Gordon House. Their frequent applause during Henry's speech led to a warning from Speaker Michael Peart against participating in the debate.

Jamaica Stock Exchange Conference

Presenter: Mike Henry, Member of Parliament – Central Clarendon
Date: Wednesday, January 22, 2014[4]
Topic: ***The right to a remedy and reparation for victims of gross human rights violation***

Greetings

As I rise to address the theme "The right to a remedy and reparation for victims of gross human rights violation", I start by visiting the words:

1. Remedy – to put or set right, straighten out, resolve, correct, repair, mend.
2. Reparation – to make amends for a wrong one has done; keeping those who have been wronged; financial reparation to victims; restitution; redress; atonement.
3. Human rights – moral principles that set out certain standards of human behaviour and are regularly protected.

[4] This speech has been reproduced verbatim from my notes and has not been edited in any way to maintain its authenticity. The speech was delivered before the parliamentary decision on January 27, 2015.

The topic I have been given then is not of my choosing but is synonymous with my political life and most timely and important to Jamaica especially as it comes at a critical time in our social and economic life.

I must commend the Jamaica Stock Exchange (JSE) for its enlightened thinking and being the first such important economic body to recognise what a game changer the achievement of reparation will be to our country and by extension the Caribbean.

As my presentation unfolds, I will proffer the positioning and practice of slavery, align my approach to this long battle over one aspect of slavery i.e. British - Caribbean chattel slavery and finally what will we use it for - the economics of it. I leave this impact to be assessed by others more economically learned than I.

While I stand ready to ensure the hopes of the people and their lack of trust and faith in leadership will be protected.

The practice of slavery, but more so in this case chattel slavery, has always been rooted in political and economic considerations. So too was emancipation and the same is true for the issue of reparations. Moral considerations evolving over generations of changing social mores and political realities have given rise to the views that have strengthened the imperative for reparations. The best known would be the holocaust.

Whatever the motive, however, the realities are inescapable that injury was done, that relief is justified, and since the injury cannot be reversed, that monetary compensation is the only true and lasting available relief that can be adjudicated. This view leapfrogs the unnecessary arguments of whether injury was done and takes us straight to the point of how to make best use of the relief provided by monetary compensation.

Slavery started with economic and political considerations. The British, Spanish, Dutch and Portuguese among other imperial powers in the new world perceived slavery along these lines of political and economic imperatives. Emancipation was acceded to on political lines with economic considerations in the forefront of the discussions certainly as evidenced by the actions of the British government in the early 19th century. Slave companies were formed, shares were taken up by tailors and traders, ships hired and staffed, insurance companies and religious bodies involved - all led by the slave trading companies of the country.

It is therefore inescapable that the search for justice through reparation be founded in political considerations by way of the political decisions required of the sovereign parliaments of the injured nations and in the economic (monetary) demands, which can be the only true measure of relief that ensures benefit to the generations ahead. These considerations allow for reparation for injuries from the crimes of war inflicted in the forced removal of a people from their native homeland, from the human rights abuses of the Middle Passage and the plantation process which ensued, and from the wholesale abandonment of the newly freed chattel turned humans embodied in the emancipation proclamation.

The stupidity of the argument of the well-treated and educated slave and the beneficial heritage of an education system, a justice system and a civil service bureaucracy, proffered by some as mitigation, must not be allowed to dignify the classing of humans as animals (chattel) and the horrors of slavery; nor must it dilute the demands for relief. The claim must be pressed not just on behalf of the ghosts of the past, but on behalf of the generations yet unborn.

It has taken nearly 200 years to reach this position on reparation as a people and as a political policy. The time is here for the reconciliation of the oral, social, political and economic accounts between the injured and those who inflicted injury. This reconciliation must, however, be between parties acting not from individual positions defensible or indefensible, but as sovereign nations acting in moral and political unison.

The generations over the next 200 years must be the beneficiaries of our collective actions now. Reparation must provide a lasting patrimony for the generations of the future who will see that, on both sides, their future unlike the past was not impacted on individually by 'us or them', but was secured by 'we' who acted collectively in the spirit of moral rectitude and political will.

It has always been my view that reparation is due from Great Britain for chattel slavery in the Caribbean and more specifically for the economic exploitation of the slave labour used through various economic means by the slave trading countries (including the African countries). All of which transcended every form of of human rights; from the forcible removal to alien countries by trickery, kidnapping, coercion and the subsequent acts of murder, rape, [miscegenation, etc.]

I quote from my book Many Rivers to Cross:
"I wish immediately, Mr. Speaker, on this subject, to refute from a personal perspective any arguments that they, the British, gave us an educational structure, for, Mr.Speaker, what they gave us was an elitist model meant to educate along the divide and rule concept, an educational content which carried with it content that did not reflect us or our solutions, and failed to impart the dignity of our African ancestry. Achievements, but left us looking outside of ourselves for our ancestry. A concept and belief, still subscribed to 'till today and manifested in the coverage and support we get from the entrenched planter class. Mr. Speaker, you cannot give me something which is my right to own."

They said by the sweat of our brow you shall eat; not by the use of your brain to think, ye hewers of wood and drawers of water The Office of United Nation High Commissioner for Human Rights website states that "All human rights are indivisible, whether they are civil and political rights, such as the right to life, equality before the law and freedom of expression; economic, social and cultural rights, such as the rights to work, social security and education, or collective rights, such as the rights to development and self-determination, are indivisible, interrelated and interdependent. The improvement of one right facilitates advancement of the others. Likewise, the deprivation of one right adversely affects the others."

Over the years, the right to reparation for Jamaica has been denied to all of us as victims through many forms of contrived barriers. Such as who is responsible for settling this abuse and debt?

Is it the state of Great Britain or the direct beneficiaries i.e. the citizens who traded?

It was a law so how can we ask present day citizens to pay?

That is now passed as at one time we did not have who benefited.

Now we have (I refer to Beckles' book and research).

Then we had the argument who are descendants; an obvious divide and rule ploy;

It wasn't me (Shaggy).

I say we all are descendants so it goes to the government for all the people; not unlike the payments to the state of Israel for the holocaust.

Indeed all of this is in my many speeches in Parliament and recorded in my book ***Many Rivers to Cross***.

As I have said earlier, counter arguments have been proposed as to benefits retained from chattel slavery; namely:

1. Language: (Admit to its economic benefits but!)
2. Jurisprudence: Look at justice today in Jamaica and murder rate and therefore let us value them and take them off the final value of my claim.

I repeat then my approach is steeped in the political and economic decision taken by the British government, in their Parliament in 1833, when they politically admitted that slavery, which was banned in their country; also extended to chattel slavery in the Caribbean as it was inhumane and abused the human rights of the slaves.

Those arguments are there and clearly indicts the whole abuse of rights; in what is the greatest abuse of human rights; exploitation of labour and of 'man's inhumanity to man'.

By this very act there leaves no more need in my mind to satisfy our right to a remedy.

Following on that act of abolition, the Caribbean slave owners lobbied and received compensation from Great Britain in the sum of £20m for loss of economic benefits to them. The slaves received nothing except a reprimand to be good 'boys and girls', grow what you need to eat on Free Villages, don't become vagrants; and mother England will take care of you; as will our absentee landlords.

For me, then as the world focused on human rights, of all kind and as Great Britain fails to apologize and settle its debt by itself or through its identified citizens.

We need a political decision by our Parliament that we have a right to a remedy and a right to this claim. There has never been a political decision by any Caribbean Parliament.

This must come through a Parliamentary decision and political vote that we have a right to pursue this claim for reparation.

Our Reparations committee. Report (to follow)

I still await a copy, but I am told.........

CARICOM 's decision

And after this what?

Use of economic benefits

For my part, as I have recorded in my book (***Many Rivers to Cross***, LMH Publishing Ltd, 2013).

I have (firstly) narrowly focused on the British chattel slave in the Caribbean and the indisputable historical fact that it was Great Britain's Parliament which abolished slavery in 1833 and responded to a political lobby on behalf of the Caribbean plantation owners, who based on their argument, that it was Britain who legitimized chattel slavery for economic and political reasons and it was Britain who sold the slaves to the Caribbean planters who now said to the planters that the slaves must be freed and yet gave newly freed class no rights of their own (freed slaves were not allowed to own titled land).

For this, the slave owners demanded compensation from the British government for each slave owned at the time of abolition. This was agreed to by the then British government and was assessed and a value of twenty million pounds (£20m) was assessed on the lost chattel slave labour. This amount was paid to the Slave owners.

As one of the beneficiaries of this payout ***"TV chef Ainsley Harriott, who had slave-owners in his family on his***

grandfather's side, said he was shocked by the amount paid out by the government to the slave owners. He went on to say that "you would think the government would have given at least some money to the freed slaves who need to find homes and start new lives. It seems a bit barbaric. It's like the rich protecting the rich. "(The Independent, February 24, 2013, *Britain's colonial shame: slave-owners given huge payouts after abolition*)

I have argued this case for all my life. Advocating that the country of the descendants of the slaves is entitled to receive the same amount of money, but at today's value (estimated by the committee to be £7.5 trillion for the Caribbean), that was paid to the slave owners and this is on behalf of all the descendants of slaves; [need] I remind us that three of our National heroes were murdered and martyred for this fight.

I have further requested that it be paid to the Government of Jamaica, for the people of Jamaica.

The matter, which is also now being taken up by Caricom, brings the other 5 Caribbean countries into the claim; with a requirement for them to make a political decision also.

When such a political decision is made; it then opens the door for Jamaica and the other Caribbean countries to take the matter to the International Court of Justice to pursue other reparation claims against all the countries who were involved in the slave trade for other forms of abuses be they - genocide, rape, murder and the host of the abuse of human rights under slavery.

I am not sure what the ultimate real monetary value of the freed chattel slaves would be but in the report coming out of The National Reparations Committee the committee talks of Jamaica's share being £2.2 trillion. Perhaps it is the audacity of the claim and or the magnitude of this part of our reparations claim; why astonishingly to me I should be asked, by so many sectors of our society; can they pay? Will they pay?

Rather than what I know should be the question; based on my own firm beliefs in this non-partisan political call:

- How will we coalesce around this matter as a conscience approach?

- How will we accept payment?
- How will it be used to transform our society?
- What must we the people put in place by even a referendum as to what we must use it for?
- It will certainly eliminate all our debt; what then?

Would the people want it be used to grant a Tax Free holiday for say 20 years to all citizens and/investors while the government prioritizes:

1. Education
2. Land titling
3. Health
4. National registration of citizens
5. Infrastructure

One thing I know I will fight for is a sum to be set aside to facilitate REPATRIATION to Africa.

The economic pundit are saying that much of the world's projected growth is predicated to be out of Africa, one can see this, and I share this view. What concerns me as I look at the movement of Spanish citizens since the economic downturn in Europe is that the skilled engineers, architects and university trained which are part of the growing unemployed are now relocating for opportunities in their former colonies.

Before I close, let me read excerpts from a recent article by the Independent Newspaper, entitled **Britain's colonial shame: Slave-owners given huge payouts after abolition:**

The true scale of Britain's involvement in the slave trade has been laid bare in documents revealing how the country's wealthiest families received the modern equivalent of

billions of pounds in compensation after slavery was abolished.
The previously unseen records show exactly who received what in payouts from the Government when slave ownership was abolished by Britain - much to the potential embarrassment of their descendants. Dr. Nick Draper from University College London, who has studied the compensation papers, says as many as one-fifth of wealthy Victorian Britons derived all or part of their fortunes from the slave economy.
As a result, there are now wealthy families all around the UK still indirectly enjoying the proceeds of slavery where it has been passed on to them. Dr. Draper said: "There was a feeding frenzy around the compensation."

The British government paid out £20m to compensate some 3,000 families that owned slaves for the loss of their "property" when slave ownership was abolished in Britain's colonies in 1833. This figure represented a staggering 40 per cent of the Treasury's annual spending budget and, in today' terms, calculated as wage values, equates to around £16.5bn.

CLOSING

And so in closing, I noticed I preceded the Logistics Hub discussions, what I as the Minister of Transport call -

An Integrated Multi-modal Development.

Which I was always intending that funds for reparations would drive the development (SHOW PLAN)

The core of this plan was air development, Vernamfield and the Railway. As such, it was my intention that we could utilize our claim shares in and resulting funds to move this and so many other investments.

For without a Sea-Air connection we are just another port and logistics needs the speed of air for delivery from factory to consumer and back to factory.

Finally, let us hope that this is the forerunner of re-engineering the social structure of Jamaica. Let us hope that the national registration of individuals, a Bill still lying fallow in the House, which will give the dignity of an identity to persons, will be readdressed. Let us hope that what we recognize is that the revolution that we require is one which makes the people recognize the responsibility of leadership, but equally responsibility of those being led.

Let us be quite clear, as I am reminded, the Haitians who became the first free black country, paid the French for their freedom. The French willingly accepted it.

In our case, the planters were paid $20m, that is a fixed sum. All I am asking for is the same $20m paid over the years of slavery that we have not been paid. Whatever that comes to, pay it to the state. Let the state then elect an enlightened government which will use it to free the minds of all of us. To let us understand there is a oneness of purpose and commitment, which is Jamaica, with the pride and dignity to lead the world. And let us in so doing, recognize that we have to be the vanguard.

Notes Among Parliamentarians

Mike,

I did see the email but was satisfied that it was an error. The members who indicated an intention to speak includes Charles/ Grange/ Baugh and the Leader.[5]

Derrick

Mike

I did see the email ~~but~~ was satisfied that it was an error.

The members who indicated an intention to speak includs Charles/ Grange/ Baugh and the Leader

Derrick

---

[5] A note exchanged between Parliamentary colleagues Derrick Smith and Mike Henry during the debate on the latter's Private Member's Motion in Parliament calling for Reparation from Britain for the atrocities of chattel slavery in the Caribbean centuries ago.

Mike,

You are right. The debate, having been opened by you, continues.

Mrss: L. B. Smith, D. K. Duncan, Paul Buchanan, Glen Broomfield and Raymond Pryce (on our side) will speak next week, Nov. 11. The Minister of Culture will make her contribution on Nov. 18 when we expect you will close the debate and members will be invited to vote.

Phillip.

Leader –
Baugh –
Bobby –
Pearnel –

Mike,

You are right. The debate, having been opened by you, continues.

Messrs. L. B. Smith, D. K. Duncan, Paul Buchanan, Glen Broomfield and Raymond Pryce (on our side) will speak next week, Nov. 11. The Minister of Culture will make her contribution on Nov. 18 when we expect you will close the debate and members will be invited to vote.[6]

Phillip

---

6. Note from Phillip Paulwell, Leader of Government Business in the House, to Central Clarendon Member of Parliament, Mike Henry, on the debate on the latter's Private Member's Motion in Parliament calling for Reparation from Britain for the atrocities of chattel slavery in the Caribbean centuries ago.

Media

The local and international press has been delving into the reparation struggle for years, generally in support of the call for justice for the horrors of British slavery, or reporting on the gradually defenceless position on the British government's official stance on the matter so far.

Among the more notable media outputs in either direction over the years were the following:

The UK Mail, 2018:

The Mail reported that back in 2008, then United States President, Barack Obama, said he did not support reparation to the descendants of slaves, something which was noted to be going against the views of around two dozen members of the US Congress who actually sponsored legislation to create a commission on slavery.

In the same year, the US House of Representatives apologised for slavery, with the Senate following suit in 2009, but neither body mentioned compensation.

As supporting material, the Mail cited material from a 2013 article that in a sorry history, European powers collectively shipped up to 60 million captured Africans from that continent into slavery in the Caribbean and the Americas.

The article zeroes in on Portuguese traders who built sub-Saharan Africa's first permanent slave trading post at Elmina in 1492.

The post is said to have later passed into Dutch and English hands, and by the 18th century they shipped tens of thousands of Africans a year through 'the door of no return' onto squalid slave ships bound for plantations in the west.

Under their modus operandi, European traders would sail to the west coast of Africa with manufactured goods which they exchanged for people captured by African traders.

The European merchants would then cross the Atlantic with ships full of slaves on the notorious 'Middle Passage'.

The travelling conditions were so torrid that many of the captives, who often had barely any space to move, did not survive the journey.

Those who made the voyage were destined to work on plantations that produced products such as sugar or tobacco for consumption back in Europe.

By the end of the 18th century campaigners called for the abolition of the trade, but this was fiercely opposed because it was so profitable.

After years of campaigning by anti-slavery activists like politician William Wilberforce, Britain banned the trade in slaves from Africa on March 25, 1807.

Slavery itself was not outlawed by Britain for another generation, in 1833, and the transatlantic trade continued under foreign flags for many years.

Some estimates say as many as 60 million people were shipped into bondage.

EURACTIV, 2014

The news service reported on the perspectives of a noted academic, whose position was against the payment of reparation.

"There is no legal basis for a claim for reparation," Robert A. Sedler, a professor at Wayne State University Law School, said.

"Slavery was legal at the time, and international law was not a part of the law of the European states. Moreover, a long period of time has passed, and all the victims of slavery are long dead," he added.

The EURACTIV article noted that some reparation cases have popped up in the United States over the last decade, but no one has been awarded compensation by that country.

However, despite his stated personal position, Sedler conceded that if negotiations are opened by European nations, they "might decide to apologise for slavery, and to provide some financial assistance to the Caribbean nations."

For instance, it was suggested that CARICOM could seek to work with the European states to set up museums for Caribbean culture and history, which would entail decisions on financing.

The legal strategy rests on the fact that the European states that are being targeted by CARICOM have all signed the International Convention on the Elimination of All Racial Discrimination, which makes it mandatory to do all in their power to eradicate racial discrimination.

The article said the Caribbean effort was then being led by Ralph Gonsalves, Prime Minister of St. Vincent and the Grenadines, who had doggedly pursued the issue for years up to that time.

Precedent?

It was pointed out that when Gonsalves found out in 2013 that London's High Court had ordered the British government to pay compensation to survivors of Kenya's Mau Mau uprising, he contacted Martyn Day, whose law firm Leigh Day represented the Mau Mau.

The British government paid £19.9 million ($33 million) to 5,228 survivors of torture during Kenya's 1950s Mau Mau uprising, and formally acknowledged that "Kenyans were subject to torture and other forms of ill treatment and that these abuses took place and that they marred Kenya's progress towards independence."

Gonsalves said slavery so traumatised the society in Caribbean countries that they have still not fully recovered.

It was noted that the reparation claim in the Caribbean takes into account what its authors say are slavery-related chronic diseases, such as hypertension and Type 2 diabetes, widespread illiteracy, the lack of museums and research centres for Caribbean history, the lack of respect for African culture and identity, continuing psychological effects of centuries of slavery, and the lack of scientific and technical know-how to compete in the global economy.

It was reported that in December 2013, the CARICOM Reparation Commission decided on six factors for the claim: public health, education, cultural institutions, cultural deprivation, psychological trauma, and scientific and technological backwardness.

The article said the international convention against discrimination requires that significant attempts should be made to solve matters amicably, but if no resolution is reached, the Caribbean nations can take their case to the International Court of Justice.

Africa Feeds, January 2020:

Africa Feeds reported in January 2020 that Ghanaian-born British lawmaker, Bell Ribeiro-Addy, has asked the UK government to, as a matter of urgency, cancel all debts owed it by its former colonies.

The Labour Member of Parliament for Streatham, who was then recently elected into the British Parliament, also said the UK government should return items that were forcefully taken from the former colonies.

She described this move as necessary to rectify its history as slave masters and compensate for the impact of colonisation and slavery.

Bell Ribeiro-Addy has said that the British government has not shown enough real remorse for acts like slavery during the colonial days.

It was noted that in 2018 when Prince Charles visited Ghana, he described the slave trade as shameful and said he hopes it doesn't recur.

While the British royal said at the time that "Britain can be proud that it led the way in the abolition of this shameful trade", he added that Britain must "have a shared responsibility to ensure that the abject horror of slavery is never forgotten".

Bell Ribeiro-Addy said that the British government must do more.

"I am someone who firmly believes that the only way you can tackle an issue is at its very root. And the racism which I and many others in this country face on a daily basis has its very root in these injustices.

"Not only will this country not apologise, but they also have not once offered a form of reparation. People see reparation as handing over a large sum of money, but why could we not start with it today? Simple things like fairer trade, simple things like returning items that do not belong to us, and simple things like cancelling debts that we have had paid over and over again."

The new shadow immigration minister for the Labour Party made the comments in her speech on the floor of the House of Commons.

Her tweets on the matter spoke even more pointedly:

1. "(To) tackle racism at its root we must confront the brutal legacy of the British Empire. Apologise and make meaningful reparation for the historic wrongs of slavery & colonialism."

2. "How can I be an equal in Parliament if this is how Parliament treats people that look just like me?"

Intriguingly, an examination of global media reports on the subject of reparation from Britain for the atrocities of slavery pointed to at least 100 former British colonies all over the world. They include the United States of America, Canada, Kenya, Uganda, Ghana and Zanzibar.

Amid the outline, it has been noted that stunningly, only 10 countries worldwide have not been colonised in some way by another power over time.

Lankaweb news service, January 2020:

An article in Lankaweb cited India saying that the British Empire owes $45 trillion to Asia, Africa and South America, which need to unite to demand reparation and accountability from the once colonial masters.

In citing that 9/11 resulted in bombing, invading and occupation of Afghanistan although Afghanistan had nothing to do with 9/11, except that the invaders have remained in Afghanistan since 2001.

Similarly, it was stated that World War 2 ended in 1945, but the Allies are still hounding former Nazi officers and arresting men in their 90s, some who cannot even remember who they are or what they did, which speaks to the vengeance for revenge from the imperialist perspective.

"Isn't it about time countries of Asia, Africa, South America unite and demand acknowledgement, accountability and reparation for all the crimes (that were) committed under colonial rule?" was a question asked in the Lankaweb article.

It noted that there is no time bar for genocide, and when the United Nations High Commissioner for Refugees lavishly uses acknowledgement, accountability and reparation to demand action against smaller member countries of the UN, it is time these countries unite to demand return of justice using the same terms.

The Lankaweb article listed the 10 countries that have not been colonised as Liberia, Japan, Thailand, Bhutan, Iran, Nepal, Tonga, China, Ethiopia and Korea. It said though not completely colonised, these nations may have had some colonial victimisations.

It was also cited that there are only 22 countries of the world that Britain has not invaded at some point, therefore almost all of the countries of the world are carrying forward legacies of colonial policy, colonial victimisation and colonial destabilisations.

Clearly the grossness and longevity of the slave system would have it extremely high on the ladder of significance in terms of crimes against humanity.

Spiked-online.com (UK), September 2019:

A Spiked online article said at a Labour Party conference in 2019, Shadow Chancellor John McDonnell said Britain should make reparation for its colonial past. McDonnell reportedly pledged that “we will provide to the citizens of the Global South free or cheap access to the green technologies developed as part of our Green Industrial Revolution.”

Labour’s Dawn Butler was noted to have already raised the example of Glasgow University’s £20 million reparation scheme as a model to emulate.

From McDonnell’s speech, however, it was noted that he was offering something that does not yet exist – the spoils of Labour’s planned ‘green industrial revolution’.

The Spiked online article cited McDonnell’s offer as pretty much another pie in the sky effort to distract from the substantial responsibilities of Britain to the Caribbean people for the human tragedy that slavery represented from that point of the spectrum.

The article said in 1833, when the British government agreed to pay 20 million pounds (about a fifth of the country’s GDP at the time) to slave owners to, as they saw it, buy the slaves their freedom, the move was because the British government wanted to avoid expropriation – taking away someone’s ‘property’ – resulting in them paying reparation to the slave owners instead of the slaves!

The Express (UK), September 2019:

In an article, the Express reported that a labour shadow cabinet minister had caused controversy after saying British "banks and businesses" must pay reparation for slavery, and comparing supporters of Prime Minister Boris Johnson to members of the racist Ku Klux Klan (KKK).

The remarks were made by Dawn Butler, the Shadow Equalities Secretary, at the Labour Party conference in Brighton. Butler said the Labour Party plans to form "consultation hubs" for slavery reparation in London, Glasgow, Liverpool and Bristol, all cities historically associated with the slave trade.

She also provocatively claimed the UK far-right regard Johnson as their "leader".

In describing a section of Johnson's support, Butler said: "They may not wear pointy white hats anymore, but they are still amongst us."

Members of the KKK, a US based white supremacist group, wear white outfits complete with pointy headgear.

Butler continued: "The only thing necessary for the triumph of evil is that good people do nothing (about it)."

The Washington Post, November 2019:

The Washington Post reported about a letter that was sent to Harvard by Antigua and Barbuda Prime Minister, Gaston Browne, demanding that the university pay his country reparation "for the gains Harvard enjoyed at the expense" of Antiguan slaves.

Browne's October 30 letter to Harvard University President, Lawrence Bacow, reportedly drew a direct line from Harvard Law School's success today to the oppression of Antiguans who were enslaved by a Massachusetts-based plantation owner in the colonial era.

That plantation owner was Isaac Royall Jr, a wealthy benefactor of Harvard's very first law professorship in 1815, whose name is reportedly still attached to Harvard's distinguished Royall Professor of Law position.

"We consider Harvard's failure to acknowledge its obligations to Antigua and the stain it bears from benefiting from the blood of our people as shocking, if not immoral," Browne wrote.

His request for reparation came as numerous universities across the United States, including Harvard, have sought to reckon with their extended ties to the chattel slavery economy.

For Browne, mere acknowledgment from Harvard has not been enough. He said the university has failed to take steps to make more concrete amends with Antigua through reparation.

He contended that the university has ignored Antiguan officials' past requests to begin discussing how reparation could work. He suggested in his letter that Harvard could offer financial assistance to the University of the West Indies campus in Antigua and Barbuda.

"Reparation from Harvard would compensate for its development on the backs of our people," Browne wrote. "Reparation is not aid; it is not a gift; it is compensation to correct the injustices of the past and restore equity. Harvard should be in the forefront of this effort."

But the Harvard response has been limited to the position that: "We recognise that there is more work to be done. Indeed, Harvard is determined to take additional steps to explore this institution's historical relationship with slavery and the challenging moral questions that arise when confronting past injustices and their legacies."

Jamaica Observer, May 2019:

The Jamaica Observer newspaper reported that Minister without Portfolio in the Office of the Prime Minister, Michael Henry, reiterated his commitment to continue advocating strongly for reparation for the descendants of slaves.

"We (have) prepared the affidavit to serve on the Queen. All the issues have been addressed by the National [Council] on Reparation and it's done in my name. So, I'm waiting on the Attorney General and others to make comments on it. I can't go much further in terms of the government, except for my own personal position," he said.

Henry restated his commitment when reparation activist, Esther Stanford and President, Universal Negro Improvement Association (UNIA), Steven Golding, called on him at Jamaica House.

"I am holding the Queen responsible for having not defended my rights. The rights of the planters were admitted to and paid for from the British Treasury, but they have not yet paid the slaves, so I'm taking it a step at a time," he said.

Henry pointed out that although chattel slavery was banned in Britain, it was used to assist in the economic development of that country.

The minister said depending on the decision of the Privy Council, the matter could be taken to the highest international court of justice.

Henry recognised Stanford for her advocacy on the issue of reparation.

"I'm very pleased to pay tribute to your work and say how great it is that we have come together at this point," he said.

The (Jamaican) National Council on Reparation (NCR) was set up to receive submissions, hear testimonies, evaluate research and carry out public consultations with the aim of guiding a national response to reparation.

It is also to present recommendations for diplomatic initiatives, security considerations, education and public information required to guide the reparation process. The NCR was previously known as the National Commission on Reparation.

Henry's strong advocacy has been bolstered by Parliament's approval of his Private Member's Motion on Reparation for Slavery.

For her part, Stanford said while there are various discussions and approaches on reparation, the topic remains critical.

During the meeting, Golding suggested that an international reparation conference be held in Jamaica, to bring together stakeholders to further discuss the matter.

In the meantime, Henry presented Stanford with an autographed copy of his publication, 'Many Rivers to Cross – A Political Journey of Audacious Hope'.

Stanford was scheduled to participate in two public lectures while in Jamaica.

PJ's focus on scoring own goal instead of the real goal

THE NEED to respond to a recent perspective from former Jamaican Prime Minister, the Most Honourable P.J. Patterson, I believe, sadly reflects, to a great extent, the failure of much of the country's past leadership on critically important issues and the need, over time, for major changes to the political landscape and thinking.

In focusing on the causes of our continued challenges as a nation and in seeking to spotlight the underlying causes for the vortex of decline in which we have existed for some time, it is unfortunate that the coronavirus (COVID-19) pandemic has, tragically, entered the mix.

But amid the realities of such hugely significant developments, it should be recognised that the central cause of our failures in the past has been the failure to recognise on merit, the geo-political syndrome that has traditionally thrived on keeping the poor across the world poorer and continually exploited.

Within that context, while conceding the relevance of much of the prognosis from Mr Patterson in respect of the global implications of the COVID-19 pandemic, I find it imperative to bring some attention to an element of hypocrisy that appeared to have emerged among his pronouncements on the means to effectively combat the pandemic.

Mr Patterson rightly cited the need for a concerted global effort to battle the virus and pointed to the extreme and life-threatening challenges that the poorer countries across the world face in their bids to survive the negative consequences of the disease. But he appeared to have, in the process, demonstrated a selective positioning on a few critical realities of the global political order and its imperatives for states like Jamaica and much of the wider Caribbean.

The former prime minister, the longest-serving person in that position in Jamaica's history, urged a focus on debt forgiveness from the International Monetary Fund (IMF) for poorer states, globally, which, in principle, was a reasonable position.

Then he also urged the African Union and CARICOM to "renew international campaigns for reparative justice against the enslavement of African people and its residual consequences on affected populations in the African Diaspora".

All good again, right?

Wrong! Not in its messaging, but in its reflective application as for the record, Mr Patterson as prime minister of Jamaica for 14 unbroken years, had the best opportunity of all of Jamaica's heads of government to foster the process of reparation for the descendants of African slaves who were wantonly abused and exploited by European powers in the Caribbean centuries ago, but he was never at the forefront of the drive back then when he was at the pinnacle of his influence.

NOT A USEFUL PARTNER

I have been there front and centre on this mission, and nowhere along the way can I recall him as a useful partner or even a fervent supporter on this very long journey.

Indeed, as I prepare to release an upcoming book on my fight for reparation, with the proceeds to help fund the remainder of the fight, I personally find it heart-rending, and almost amusing in the same breath, that this giant of a political figure in Jamaica's history is only now seriously calling for a focus on the subject matter, this while conveniently pitching for debt relief for poorer countries like Jamaica when he never, from my memory, pitched for reparative justice for the Jamaican and wider Caribbean people, of whom he was one of the most recognisable leaders who, interestingly, benefited immensely from the Black Power syndrome.

It is extremely ironic that someone who had full opportunity to bring about real change for our people on a position of solid historical grounding remained pretty much silent on the issue for all his time in power and effectively failed us where and when it mattered so much but is now seeking cover behind a call for debt relief from the global financial community for the ravages of COVID-19.

Instead of going after what we are clearly owed as a nation and people, some of our past leaders, like Mr Patterson, dithered at the wheels of State, only to be now, at least in his case, batting for virtual handouts from the rich when both rich and poor countries are being, perhaps, equally devastated by the COVID-19 pandemic.

Indeed, for the records and to reinforce the point, what was Mr Patterson's contribution over his 14-year leadership span on the matter of reparation? And even when he retired but maintained a commentary focused on the country's national path, where was he, and how silent was he when, for example, then British Prime Minister David Cameron, a descendant of owners of chattel slaves, strode into Jamaica in 2015 and refused to even discuss the question of reparation with the Government and people of this country?

Yes, debt relief is quite relevant, but it has been historically used almost like a chemically created plot or tool for use by the traditional colonial masters to dangle before our leadership to keep us subservient and effectively in eternal poverty as we hang out our caps and seek what we are not owed in any clear-cut way.

This is while reparation is the exact opposite – what we are intrinsically owed based on legal, historical, economic and human right grounds. Yet people like Mr Patterson, him with all of 14 years as the team captain at the wicket, did not have the foresight or, perhaps, the backbone to fight for this right of ours!

As the saying goes, "None but ourselves can free our minds", it is important to note that continued lack of belief in ourselves as a people, stemming significantly from the examples of some of our past leaders, has been essentially to our peril as a nation and people.

While his call for debt forgiveness for poorer states globally within the increasingly challenging COVID-19 circumstances does have merit, were the gross exploitation, racial disenfranchisement, and human degradation of chattel slaves in the Caribbean not more compelling grounds for reparation? And who does not know that debt forgiveness has been a central plank of the claim for reparation.

One could reasonably ask, what would it take for the average person to reach this logical conclusion on the matter, much less a gifted mind like Mr Patterson?

But indeed, in just the same way that we insulted our forbearers and liberators, including our national heroes, in allowing David Cameron to pompously speak in our Parliament without any request or requirement of him to reference the subject of reparation, some of us as leaders continue to almost ignore what is our intrinsic right, preferring instead to panhandle on the global financial stage.

■ L. Michael Henry (Mike Henry) is member of parliament for Central Clarendon and minister without portfolio in the Office of the Prime Minister. Email feedback to michaelhenrylmh@yahoo.com.

Mike Henry's perspective on reparation amidst the challenges of the coronavirus (COVID-19) pandemic.

OPINION | 16

Mike Henry scores own goal against PJ Patterson

Delano Franklyn

MIKE Henry, minister without portfolio in the Office of the Prime Minister and Member of Parliament for Central Clarendon, wrote an article entitled, 'PJ's focus on scoring own goal instead of the real goal', which was published in the Sunday Observer on May 10, 2020 and the *Sunday Gleaner* on May 17, 2020.

In the article, Mr Henry criticised Mr Patterson for, "seeking to cover behind a call for debt relief from the global financial community for the ravages of Covid-19".

Mr Henry also criticised Mr Patterson for "remaining silent" during his 14 years as prime minister on the issue of reparative justice.

Mr Henry, who used his article

and many others who have also been "front and centre" of the reparations movement in Jamaica.

Mr Henry's article was in response to a policy document issued by Mr Patterson on April 22, 2020 in his capacity as statesman in residence at the PJ Patterson Centre for Afro-Caribbean Policy Advocacy which is based at The University of the West Indies.

In the policy document, Mr Patterson outlined the impact that the COVID-19 pandemic is having on the Caribbean and in African countries, and suggested that a multilateral response was required. He called on the African Union and Caricom to demand, among other things, debt can-

Patterson and Reparations

Ambassador Emeritus Audley Rodriques, in an article which was published in the *Sunday Observer* on May17, 2020 pointed out numerous instances of the support given by Mr Patterson when he was prime minister, to the call for reparations.

I wish to add a few other actions by Mr Patterson which clearly shows that he was not "silent" on reparations as Mr Henry would wish for us to believe.

Mr Patterson gave full instructions to his minister of foreign affairs and the Ministry of Foreign Affairs to prepare for Jamaica's full and total participation in the World Conference against Racism, Racial Discrimination, Xenophobia and Related Intolerance which was held in South Africa from August 31 to September 8, 2001. This conference was extremely significant in advancing the international debate on reparations.

Mr Patterson also gave his full

HENRY...accused P J Patterson of not scoring real goal

PATTERSON...taken to task b[y] Henry

Mr Henry also claimed that Mr Patterson remained silent on the reparations issue when former prime minister of the UK, David Cameron, visited and spoke in the Jamaican parliament in 2015. This is simply not true.

It was Mr Patterson who issued a stinging rebuke to Mr Cameron's suggestion "to forget the historical past and move on together to build for the future". How could Mr Patterson's denunciation of slavery, "as a most

countries".

On March 4,1994 at a c ference on Financing Caribbean, held in Mont Bay, he called for "further c and debt service reduction some of the countries of region".

On September 25, 1997 in address to the United Nati 52nd General Assembly, pointed out, "that the d burden remains a major c straint on development".

A rebutal of Mr. Henry's perspective on reparation amidst the challenges of the coronavirus (COVID-19) pandemic.

FRANK PHIPPS

Frank Phipps is a member of the National Council for Reparation. The views expressed here are not stated on behalf of the council. Send comments to the Jamaica Observer or frank.phipps@yahoo.com.

Magical dreams and uncertain destiny — A response

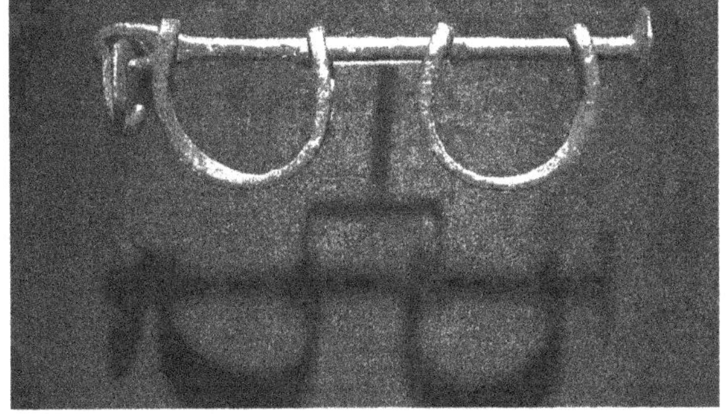

The former enslaved people in the Caribbean have struggled for better to come after the empty freedom at Emancipation.

CHRISTOPHER Burns has joined the debate on the call for reparation with an article in last week's The Agenda in the Sunday Observer (May 17) without come down on either side for the merits of the call — somewhat like a referee at a no-contest event, involving Mike Henry and P J Patterson, where both make the call. However, we must welcome his public statement as the views of a self-proclaimed agnostic, where silence can hurt the cause and whispered reasons for non-belief could be even more damaging.

Burns joins the transnational dispute with an opening ploy, stating, "History is for arguing." Despite the rhetorical brilliance of some of the arguments put forward in favour of reparation by prominent scholars, reparation is not a panacea and cannot guarantee human harmony, neither will payment of whatever amount create happiness in ways that love or simple laughter can. No doubt, Professor Verene Shepherd and others may wish to comment on this statement that history is for arguing.

Without rushing into that argument where more qualified people will tread, it is necessary to quote from the article itself to show what history has turned up: "Whether one agrees with the unlikelihood of reparation payments happening in this century, or the next, the awareness is helpful. Furthermore, understanding the pangs of the transatlantic slave trade, with its attendant indignity and cruel contempt for human life, makes it criminally boring for anyone with a conscience to ignore the message of reparation. This is so because the basis for reparation is cast on years of extensive research, scholarly legal arguments, and evidence of lingering sociocultural subjugation. Centuries of resource extraction, exploitation, free labour, and myriad other disgusting crimes against humanity have left signs of the hellish reality of wide-scale poverty, malnutrition, disease, hunger, inadequate shelter, and food insecurity all over, but disproportionately among Africans and descendants of African slaves."

That said, there can be no better way for stating the reasons for seeking reparation to correct the injuries of the past — a call for action to make amends for the wrongs that were done. Nevertheless, Burns cautions us not to allow the awfulness of history to cause us to harbour unrealistic expectations and useless fairy tale dreams at the expense of taking the request steps for self-improvement. One can take issue with that advice, for cautious inaction is where the article deals with the "what" and the "how" for reparation without thought for the "why" — what being evils of slavery and how is the cash payment for making amends.

Having dealt with what he calls the magical dream for reparation, Burns owes your readers Part 2 with his views on "why" reparation; the uncertain destiny he proclaims. Part 2 follows naturally from his closing paragraph: "Sensibly speaking, we have to create an enabling society that gives an opportunity to all." This looks to the future for reparation without the dead hand of caution.

> Black people everywhere have too long been deprived of equal opportunities for shelter, health care, education, and jobs; this is why reparation is necessary to correct the persistent wrong-headedness in the concept of humanity that excludes black people. Black skin should not make a difference when creating "an enabling society that gives equal opportunities for all"

The dark tunnel for travelling to the future is obstructed by what the late Professor Fred Hickling calls the European delusion of white supremacy in the Caribbean from the late 15th century with a claim to all therein as his, in his book *Owning our Madness*. The delusion of white supremacy was practised worldwide where the people from Europe were plundering the natural resources of other countries and decimating the indigenous people with the greatest wickedness in the Americas and the Caribbean for people of African origin who suffered double cruelty by forcible abduction from their home followed by chattel slavery on the plantations.

Black people everywhere have too long been deprived of equal opportunities for shelter, health care, education, and jobs; this is why reparation is necessary to correct the persistent wrong-headedness in the concept of humanity that excludes black people. Black skin should not make a difference when creating "an enabling society that gives equal opportunities for all".

The former enslaved people in the Caribbean have struggled for better to come after the empty freedom at Emancipation. Starting with a handicap from degradation and deprivation they lifted up themselves by the bootstrap — those who had boots — to get where they are today. More still needs to be done for this and succeeding generations to enjoy a better quality of life with a level playing field, where no one is denied opportunities because of the colour of that person's skin.

This is what reparation is about, those who savagely crushed the humanity of people from Africa must pay to repair it for the benefit of present and succeeding generations. Why remain an agnostic by closing eyes to the light of truth and justice for the people of African descent?

A scholarly perspective from Queen's Counsel Frank Phipps on reparation amidst the challenges of the coronavirus (COVID-19) pandemic.

THE SUNDAY OBSERVER May 24, 2020 twitter/jamaicaobserver www.jamaicaobserver.com

FRANK PHIPPS

Frank Phipps, QC, is a member of the National Council on Reparation. Send comments to the Jamaica Observer or frank.phipps@yahoo.com.

Racism and slavery, like a horse and carriage?

RACISM cannot be removed from a bigot's mind, especially when the worst bigots are asymptomatic. What can be done is not tolerate it.

The practice of racism was brought to national and international attention by the recent George Floyd incident in the US that sparked demonstrations in protest demanding change as the answer to racial discrimination. All well-thinking Jamaicans support actions in the USA for change as the answer to racism because Jamaicans know the atrocities inflicted on human beings during the period of British rule, with racial discrimination leaving consequences that must now be undone as a just cause for reparation.

Four centuries ago the head of State for one of the leading nations that practised racism when trafficking in people from Africa, Queen Elizabeth I, had condemned the practice before Britain was involved, as reported by Thomas Clarkson notes 1785:

"The first importation of slaves from Africa, by our countrymen, was in the reign of Elizabeth, in the year 1562. The Queen was greatly concerned about these events: She [Elizabeth I] seems to have been aware of the evils to which its continuance might lead, or that, if it were sanctioned, the most unjustifiable means might be made use of to procure the persons of the natives of Africa.

"Summoning Captain John Hawkins, to brief her regarding his voyage to Africa, the Queen: expressed her concern, lest any of the Africans should be carried off without their free consent, declaring that: 'It would be detestable, and call down the vengeance of heaven upon the undertakers.' "

Disregarding Her Majesty's directive, Hawkins commenced centuries of British slave trade.

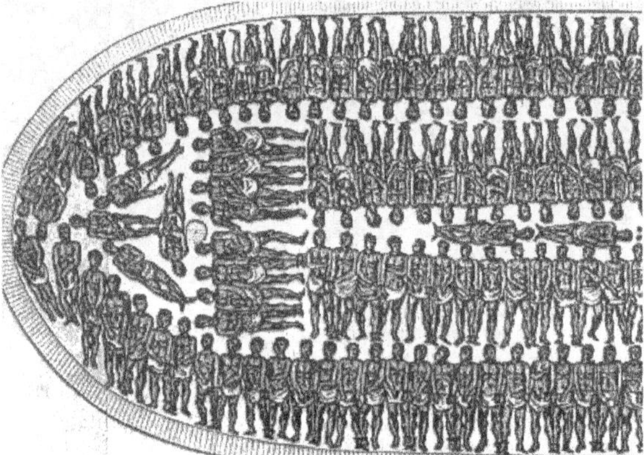

The cargo on-board the slave ships were human beings, squeezed together in close confinement as bulk load below deck in numbers as many as space will allow for maximum profit.

Being at odds with one another is the euphemism for what took place in Jamaica with a majority black population. This was a country always in turmoil with the struggle by the people from Africa against colonial rule by the white people from Britain. Many died in the revolt and more died from the reprisal that followed. We cannot close our eyes to the abuses of the people from Africa, nor turn our backs on the heroes and hundreds more who sacrificed with their lives to get us where we are today

THE DEVIL'S PARODY

Thereafter there was the most horrifying show of man's inhumanity to man, in three stages, that a devil would resent.

First, there was the kidnapping of people from Africa; the physical and emotional trauma from being forcibly seized in your homeland, taken from family and village, mercilessly bound with other victims and carried away to hell holes to await the next ship for their final confinement. These were white strangers holding black people in captivity in circumstances that could make any normal person lose his/her mind.

Next stage was the dehumanising experience on slave ships crossing the Atlantic Ocean. The cargo on-board was human beings, squeezed together in close confinement as bulk load below deck in numbers as many as space will allow for maximum profit. How long did the journey last? What were the health and hygiene practices below deck where the cargo was kept? What sustenance was provided to preserve life? The answers can be the reason some preferred suicide; and if they survived, there was always the risk of being thrown overboard to save the ship from any hazard of a sea journey, as was done for saving the *Zong* off the coast of Black River in 1781.

The final stage for the madding journey was on the plantations in the Americas and the Caribbean with the well-known cruelties of enslavement and the denial of their humanity. On arrival in the British West Indies (now Caribbean Community) their destination was the cane fields, in slavery, while their captors sang, "Britons never, never shall be slaves" or from the Empire song "Land of hope and glory, mother of the free".

TO WHOSE BENEFIT?

When we talk for reparation an issue to be considered is to what extent some of the victims in the slave trade were sold by other Africans to the white trader for filthy lucre. The business of the time was mega wealth at any price for an operation where the white planters and the black enslaved people worked together in a partnership for the best profit where one side could not do it alone. History shows how they were unequally yoked; putting them at odds with one another. When considering reparation, in the milieu of unbridled capitalism a question to be answered is whether the head of State for the West Indian colonies also shared in the revenue from slavery?

WAS SLAVERY ENTIRELY ABOUT RACISM?

On the plantations, the white partner had his fundamental rights and freedoms protected; the black partner was property of the planter like any other animal on th farm, as industrial equipmen The planter received financia benefit from the joint enter prise; the enslaved peopl worked for free.

Being at odds with on another is the euphemism fo what took place in Jamaic with a majority black pop ulation. This was a countr always in turmoil with th struggle by the people fron Africa against colonial rule b the white people from Britair Many died in the revolt an more died from the reprisa that followed. We cannot clos our eyes to the abuses of th people from Africa, nor tur our backs on the heroes an hundreds more who sacri ficed with their lives to ge us where we are today. Th important question is: Wa racism the reason or cause fo the combat between plante and slave?

A plausible test is where yo see your daughter or siste with a man from the planta tion, how would you knov whether he should be accepte as coming from the grea house or rejected coming fror the cane field? The differenc is important for maintainin the social integrity of th island. It just happened tha the black people from Afric were assigned to the can fields while the white peopl were in the great house. Tha made the difference whe nature was exploited for th colour of skin to determin who was free and who wa enslaved. The planters use that label to the fullest exter to instil a belief of superiorit for the master and inferiori ty for the enslaved individu als. This is the insanity tha demands reparation for a the people. We still mindless ly abuse each other and allov the weak to remain in depra vation without full freedor and equal opportunity for ec ucation and self-developmen

Sad to say, it will be long road for the victim of racial discrimination t travel in order to unlearn th lessons from mental slaver The recent statement fror King's House unravelling th governor general's dilemm over the hidden message c racial discrimination in hi emblem of honour is an ac for reparation. How muc further should we go topplin statues, destroying images or dispelling other form of honour now regarded a relics of colonialism in orde to achieve reparation? Hov far is enough, or too fa for the National Council o Reparation to go?

Legal Opinions on Reparation Claim

Following my repeated parliamentary insistence on keeping my Private Member's Motion on reparation alive, against all odds, including being constantly delayed by successive speakers of the House, the fact is that the motion fell off the order paper for three successive parliamentary seasons over some five years, but in the end, the motion was unanimously passed.

So having won the political war to have the motion passed, but with no subsequent positive reaction from successive governments to take the lead nationally, I had to battle from the trenches – so to speak – to keep the hope alive.

I did this through always raising the subject and pursuing all the available avenues, including from the reparatory body out of The University of the West Indies (UWI), and summoning all of my own political acumen and skill.

One such incident was my attack on the Deputy Prime Minister of the United Kingdom, who visited Jamaica years ago. In that act I deliberately imparted my consistency of purpose and belief in the fight of the Rastafarians and their belief in repatriation, and my own belief and clarity of thought as I continued to fight racism and classism and the 'cousin syndrome' of my country, much of it coupled with the cynical abuse in being called 'Brown Rasta' or 'Rasta Mike'.

I kept the motion alive by faith and belief.

I recall my visit to South Africa for World Cup Football accompanied by my wife, Dawn, and our visit to see Dudley

Thompson to discuss my continued fights, and how we exchanged our vision and I learnt of his feelings in leading the early charge for black consciousness which went back unto my own exposure to persons with whom I had shared moments and hours, the likes of: Louis Farrakhan, Stokely Carmichael, Julian Bond and Maynard Jackson, and latter years Prime Minister Ralph Gonsalves of St Vincent and the Grenadines, when we both visited Libya as guests of Muammar al-Ghaddafi.

So from that point, when the Jamaica Labour Party (JLP) became government again in 2007 to 2011, I used that period aligned with my chairmanship of the party, from which no chairman had ever apologised to the Rastas for the atrocities of the Coral Gardens' massacre in St James, with the support of then Prime Minister, Bruce Golding, to push and conclude the debate in Parliament.

Interestingly, Mr. Golding said he supported the cause for reparation, but thought I should not confine the focus to Jamaica, but seek a Caribbean unity. But I resisted that; I was always focused on the narrow point of chattel slavery, and I was aware of how the White Anglo-Saxon Protestants had penetrated the minds of our class structure right into today's 21st century.

In the way of the legal soundness of the motion and the petition to be sent to the British Monarchy, I must note the perspectives of three noted legal luminaries in Frank Phipps QC, Lord Anthony Gifford and legal consultant Lawrence Cartier in the UK.

In the case of Frank, one day I received a call from him, my political colleague, who was chairman of the JLP when I joined the party. Having refereed numerous political fights that I had with some other colleagues, including Edward Seaga, in the JLP, Frank came to my rescue many times and I consequently developed much respect for him and his solid, clear mind and thinking.

It was therefore no surprise that I chose him years later to represent the JLP in at least one major matter, and again, I suddenly received another call from Frank, in which he expressed interest in teaming with the reparation effort, to positively use a national decision in the country's interest.

With the petition having been done and clearly reflecting Frank's legal guidance and perspectives of the subject matter, and canned newspaper articles on his wider perspectives, the positions of Lord Anthony Gifford QC and Lawrence Cartier are outlined below to broaden the scope of legal viewpoints on the matter, which have combined to guide the petition and the composition of this publication:

From Lord Anthony Gifford QC:

February 7, 2019

The Honourable Olivia Grange, CD, MP
Minister of Culture, Gender, Entertainment & Sports,
4-6 Trafalgar Road,
Kingston 5

Dear Minister,

Re: Privy Council Petition

Following the meeting with you and members of the National Reparations Council on 8th November 2018. I undertook to write a letter giving you my considered opinion on the legal aspects of the proposed petition.

My concerns had been caused by having read the most recent case or a referral under section 4 of the Judicial Committee Act. which was **Chief Justice of the Cayman Islands v Judicial and Legal Services Commission** (2012) UKPC 39. The case concerned the tenure of office and the conduct of the Chief Justice. The point was raised whether the Judicial Committee had the power to decline to rule on issues raised in a Petition referred to it under section 4, in spite of the clear words of the section: "and such committee shall thereupon hear or consider the same, and shall advise Her Majesty thereon in manner aforesaid."

The Privy Council ruled that " it would be open in principle to it to advise Her Majesty that it is inappropriate to provide substantive answers....... if it considered that that is the right course to take." It mentioned in particular petitions which required "facts to be found, where there a dispute as to certain crucial facts." I thought that there was a danger that the Privy Council would find it “inappropriate" to deal with the complex history of the crimes against humanity committed against the ancestors or most Jamaicans.

I have now done some more research and it has been most enlightening. I found cases in which the Privy Council had gone at length in to historical facts, if necessary going back over centuries, in order to resolve the petition before them.

For instance in **Re States of Jersey** (1853) 9 Moo PCC 195 the question was: can the Crown by Order in Council make laws for Jersey or must all laws go through the representatives of the people of Jersey? This was a most important issue for the people of Jersey, and the Privy Council found for the people against the Government. In a long judgment the PC traced the history of Jersey back to AD 491.

But the most compelling case which I found was **Re Southern Rhodesia** [1919] AC 211. The question in issue was whether unalienated lands, including “native reserves” and “waste land” could lawfully be disposed of by the British South Africa Company (Cecil Rhodes’ company) which had exercised no rights over them. The decision involved investigating the detailed history of the dealings between Queen Victoria and King Lobengula, and whether the “natives” had acquired any rights. The Privy Council decided in favour of Rhodes’ company, thus bestowing on Rhodes vast tracts of African land and nullifying the rights of the Matabele and other peoples.

One could well ask, if the Privy Council felt able to rely on centuries of history in order to uphold the rights of the people of Jersey and Cecil Rhodes, how could they refuse to do the same with the undisputed atrocities of the transatlantic trade and chattel slavery in order to provide justice by way of reparation. Certainly in the light of these decisions the Privy Council could not say that it was “inappropriate” to advise Her Majesty on the petition.

I add that what I said at the meeting, that if these arguments are presented with the passion and eloquence that Frank has shown us, in front of a court with a public gallery packed with activists and media, the impact could be huge.

I therefore am fully in support of the petition, and not just as a symbolic gesture. Having gone back to the many cases cited in **Halsbury's Laws of England**, Fourth Edition Re-issue, Volume 10, paragraph 415 with footnotes) it is clear that the Privy Council has not hesitated to advise under section 4 on issues of major importance involving deep historical analysis.

I hope that this will be of assistance to you and the Honourable Attorney General when she is consulted by you.

With best wishes
Anthony Gifford

From Lawrence Cartier in the UK: [7]

The matters in issue are too complex to set out here in detail and will also need to be reviewed when we have sight of Counsel's Opinion, but please note the following.

There are of course substantial legal difficulties in a case of this nature even though there is a powerful moral cause. Issues of causation, remoteness, and of course passage of time, all raise potentially insurmountable legal difficulties which are also compounded by the Court generally being unwilling to create a precedent which can open the floodgates to a plethora of cases of this nature.

The crime of slavery is indisputable, but it will clearly be helpful also to establish a particular causal link to modern day under-privilege and suffering in order to seek not only an historical apology for the crimes committed but also redress and some form of comprehension.

A possible approach has been proposed by my son Adam. From his preliminary research it seems that when Jamaica became independent in 1962, the pre-existing debt, incurred during the years of British rule, was not written off. On the basis that this is correct and there has been no subsequent variation, it seems that the continuation of this debt may at least be a contributory cause to the lack of economic development of Jamaica and to the detriment suffered by its modern day citizens.

An approach to the proposed Petition could be that if at the relevant time the slaves had received compensation, in the same way as the slave owners did in 1834 (when slavery was ruled to be a crime against humanity), then the slaves would have developed their own businesses and economy in Jamaica with the result that Jamaica would have had no, or at least a substantially reduced, national debt when independence was declared in 1962.

7. This correspondence emanates from the friendship with Lawrence, Peter and I.

Alternatively, it could also be argued that that given the crimes and unremedied consequences of slavery which were suffered under British rule, the British ought to have written off the national debt or at least substantially reduced it to give the newly independent country a fair and equitable start.

The ongoing difficulties arising from the Jamaican national debt also necessitated Jamaica borrowing money from the IMF, the World Bank and the Inter-American Development Bank. It could be argued that the size of the national debt (caused by the British failure to compensate the slaves) has prevented the development of the economy for the benefit of all Jamaicans.

It may also be possible to link the above borrowing to the implementation of Structural Adjustment Policies (SAPs), which also limited Jamaica's economic development. These SAPs have apparently been instrumental in substantial Jamaican industries such as tourism, agriculture, utilities, airports, highways and bauxite all being foreign owned.

According to the US Centre for Response of Economic Policy, Jamaica is one of the most indebted countries in the world and this is at least in part because half of the tax paid by the Jamaican people goes to service their oversized national debt. By reference to the above, it may be possible for the quantum of the Petition against the British Government to be extrapolated from the size of the national debt of Jamaica at the time of independence plus interest since then, provided a causal link between the suffering of the slaves and size of the national debt can be established.

Subject to further research, it may be possible to establish along the above lines a causal link between the wrongdoings of the past and the underprivileged in Jamaican society of today. Subject to your own view and that of Counsel, it may suggest a way of presenting the Petition more solidly on the basis of a valid economic argument.

In addition to the legal claims, political pressure and media support are of course also critical. As previously discussed, it could make an enormous difference if the campaign was politically supported and fronted by a major international figure such as Usain Bolt.

Please let us see a copy of Counsel's Opinion and let us know the views of yourself and Counsel regarding the above.

Regards,
Lawrence

Previous Reparation Payments Globally

Among the most notable atrocities globally, for which reparation have been paid over time up to 2014, were the following:

The Holocaust

The closest analogue to reparation for slavery was probably the reparation that West Germany agreed to pay after the Holocaust. A major component was the $7 billion (2014 dollars) West Germany agreed to give to the then young state of Israel.

Apartheid

One of the duties of South Africa's post-apartheid Truth and Reconciliation Commission, besides investigating human rights abuses committed by the apartheid government, was recommending reparation and other policies to redress those abuses and aid victims of the former regime. The commission recommended about $360 million in reparation to be distributed in six annual payments to victims identified by the commission, but in 2003, President Thabo Mbeki announced that he would authorise only $85 million to be given in one-time payments of $3,900 (above the average annual salary in the country at that time). The recipients numbered 16,397 as of 2012, a tiny fraction of the actual number of people who were victimised by the regime.

Japanese internment

The forced internment of 120,000 Japanese-Americans in camps during World War II resulted in about $3.1 billion in property loss and $6.4 billion in income loss, in 2014 dollars. After accounting for the possibility that that money might have been invested and gotten above-inflation returns, the economic losses are even larger.

Congress made two attempts at reparation, the Japanese-American Claims Act of 1948 and the Civil Liberties Act of 1988. Between 1948 and 1965, the former authorised payments totalling $38 million (which came to somewhere between $286 to $374 million in 2014 dollars), which didn't come close to matching the economic loss.

The latter offered survivors $20,000 each in reparation.

By 1998, 80,000 survivors had collected their share, for a total pay-out of $1.6 billion (between $2.3 billion and $3.2 billion in 2014). There is no accounting by which either measure adequately repaid internees for their economic losses, let alone compensated for pain and suffering.

Forced sterilisation

Most American states practised one or another form of eugenics during the 20th century, with forced sterilisations of 'unfit' people being a prime instrument. The targets were largely but by no means entirely mentally or developmentally disabled; poor black women on welfare were especially likely to be victimised in this manner.

The Supreme Court gave the practice a green light with 1927's Buck v. Bell, and eventually 33 states adopted the practice, forcibly sterilizing about 65,000 people in total through the 1970s. Oregon forcibly sterilised people as late as 1981, and its Board of Eugenics (renamed the 'Board of Social Protection' in 1967) was only abolished in 1983.

Very few states have acknowledged or apologised for these policies, and only one, North Carolina, has set up a reparation programme. The state sterilised about 7,600 people, most of whom are no longer living, but in 2013 passed a $10 million reparation programme that should give the more than 177 living victims somewhere in the range of $50,000 each. The payments should have been made within a few years.

Some of the victims objected, saying the proposed payment did not come. As one victim, Elaine Riddick Jessie (who was sterilised at age 14 after being raped and giving the resulting son up for adoption), said, "If I accepted it, what kind of value am I putting on my life?"

California, which sterilised by far the largest number of people of any state, did not pay out reparation up to 2014.

Tuskegee experiment

After the end of the Tuskegee experiment — in which 399 black men with syphilis were left untreated to study the progression of the disease between 1932 and 1972 — the government reached a $10 million out-of-court settlement with the victims and their families in 1974, which included both monetary reparation (in 2014 dollars, $178,000 for men in the study who had syphilis, $72,000 for heirs, $77,000 for those in the control group and $24,000 for heirs of those in the control group) and a promise of lifelong medical treatment for both participants and their immediate families. According to the CDC, 15 descendants were still receiving treatment through the programme in 2014.

Rosewood

In 1923, the primarily black town of Rosewood on the Gulf Coast of Florida was destroyed in a race riot that, by official counts, killed at least six black residents and two whites (though some descendants of the town's residents have claimed many more were killed and dumped in mass graves).

In 1994, the state of Florida agreed to a reparation package worth around $3.36 million in 2014 dollars, of which $2.4 million in 2014 would be set aside to compensate the 11 or so remaining survivors of the incident, $800,000 to compensate those who were forced to flee the town, and $160,000 would go to college scholarships primarily aimed at the descendants.

The Way Forward

It is not a question of if Britain will agree on a process of reparation for the descendants of slaves in the Caribbean, but when this process of resolution will be accepted and over what period will it be implemented, what forms of compensation and developmental initiatives will be involved, and how far will it all go in terms of closing the chapter on the horrific slave experiences between Africa and the Caribbean.

But just like how the University of Glasgow has agreed to and jointly charted a course of reparation with The University of the West Indies to the tune of £20 million, applicable primarily in developmental initiatives over a number of decades, it is similarly realistic that a broad British reparation package would be centred significantly on the development agenda across the Caribbean.

Having undeniably exploited the region's economies and its imported human capital to its benefit, the British Empire now has a number of possible options which have been generally deemed applicable and appropriate to be part of an overall reparation package for the Caribbean, ultimately from more than just Britain, and including other European powers that were similarly engaged in the slave trade to, and slavery in the Caribbean, centuries ago.

Among the proposed options are:

1. A full and formal apology accepting responsibility, committing to non-repetition and pledging to repair the harm that has been caused by the slave system. Statements of regret only are not good enough.

2. Indigenous people development programmes, with the former colonising European states taking on responsibility to support these programmes.

3. Funding for repatriation and resettlement of persons desirous of returning to Africa, including the issues of citizenship and re-integration.

4. The establishment of cultural institutions and the return of cultural heritage to right the wrongs of systematic destruction of the cultural identities and language of the indigenous people, the enslaved Africans and the indentured workers.

5. Addressing and remedying the public health crisis in the Caribbean through the injection of more modern science, technology and capital generally into the systems within the region.

6. Education programmes to bolster the efforts of the Caribbean region to catch up with the world, having inherited a flawed and inadequate system built on structural discrimination, which has hampered the drive for social and economic development regionally.

7. Debt for equity arrangements in support of the developmental agenda.

8. The enhancement of historical and cultural knowledge exchanges to help correct centuries of disconnection and restore greater pride among the people of the Caribbean region and rebuild 'bridges of belong'.

9. Psychological rehabilitation after the inter-generational transmission of trauma. The history of colonialism by European states has generally inflicted serious psychological trauma on indigenous and African descendant people, who now need rehabilitation for their affected population, including mental health issues and some other manifestations of illness.

10. The right to development through the use of technology. For centuries, the trade and production of Europe could be summed up in the British slogan: "Not a nail is to be made in the colonies". That was a deliberate decision to retard the technology available for development within Caribbean states. Technology transfer and science sharing for development is therefore an important part of repairing the deliberate harm to the development prospects of Caribbean countries.

11. Debt cancellation and monetary compensation. Caribbean countries which emerged from slavery have inherited the massive crisis of community poverty and inability to adequately deal with the development of the respective countries because of the burdens of the legacy of colonialism. In the efforts to overcome those challenges, such states have racked up onerous levels of debt, which rightly belong to a great extent to the colonial states which made no meaningful attempt to deal with the debilitating legacy of colonialism.

12. Support for the payment of domestic debt, the cancellation of international debt, and direct monetary payments, where appropriate, are necessary reparatory actions to genuinely correct the harm caused by colonialism.

A reparation package that considered all of the above and incorporated most of the proposals, would go a far way to lay the sort of foundation that would allow for the gradual acceptance of the harsh realities and adequate emotional acceptance of the harsh realities and indignity of the slave system which, as Prince Charles said, should not be forgotten, even when possibly forgiven.

Hon. Frank Phipps, OJ, QC

It is with profound gratitude and respect that I laud the invaluable input of my longtime friend and intellectual political colleague, legal luminary Hon. Frank Phipps, OJ, QC, who prepared the petition to be sent to the British Government and Monarchy.

Frank, which is how I personally address him despite my awe of appreciation of his pretty amazing legal capacity and astuteness even at his present age, was notably the Chairman of the Jamaica Labour Party (JLP) when I entered the political fray locally. Hence my reverence for him as a solid foundational figure who has withstood the challenges of time and charted one of the most illustrious legal careers in Jamaica and the wider region.

Having worked closely together over decades in politics with critical reference to the legal parameters, it was such an overwhelming feeling when in little time after being contacted on the matter, Frank consented to produce the affidavit for presentation to the powers that be in Britain.

This giant of a man has since helped to springboard the fight for reparatory justice from Britain to virtually the front steps of Buckingham Palace and 10 Downing Street, and simple gratitude is nowhere near enough for an oh so critical input from the Queen's Counsel.

Added to that, over the years, Frank has also sought to drum home the point that Britain needs to step up and accept responsibility for its callous and dark deeds in fostering the system of chattel slavery in the Caribbean, including Jamaica, centuries ago.

With his submissions and consequent conclusions leaving pretty much no wiggle room for the defence, the outcome of the case for reparation from Britain is far more about 'how soon', rather than 'if'.

I take a bow in honour of and with due respect to my great friend and longtime intellectual colleague, Hon. Frank Phipps, OJ, QC.

Letters to Ministers

(Correspondence is ongoing)

MIKE HENRY, OJ, CD, MP.
CENTRAL CLARENDON

HOUSES OF PARLIAMENT
GORDON HOUSE,
DUKE STREET,
KINGSTON, JAMAICA
TELEPHONE: (876)938-0005
CELLPHONE: (876) 286-0740
FAX: (876)759-8752
EMAIL: michaelhenrylmh@yahoo.com

December 15, 2020

Marlene Malahoo Forte, MP, QC, JP
1st Floor North Tower,
NCB Towers,
2 Oxford Road
Kingston 5

Dear Attorney General,

RE: Referral of Petition to Her Majesty for Reparation for Enslavement

I attach hereto proposed Petition for Reparation for your information and support. The documentation was shared with the National Council on Reparation that was mandated by Parliament to recommend citation for reparation.

It is my intention to continue the way forward by further education of our people on their rights and what remedies available to them for reparation by the launch of my book in January 2021 and may need to expand our discussions.

I am pleased to submit an unedited copy of the title:

Reparation – "Pay us What You Owe Us."

Thank you for your assistance and your readiness to always give your support.

Regards,
Central Clarendon

L. Michael Henry, OJ, CD, MP
Member of Parliament

MIKE HENRY, OJ, CD, MP.
CENTRAL CLARENDON

HOUSES OF PARLIAMENT
GORDON HOUSE,
DUKE STREET,
KINGSTON, JAMAICA
TELEPHONE: (876)938-0005
CELLPHONE: (876) 286-0740
FAX: (876)759-8752
EMAIL: michaelhenrylmh@yahoo.com

December 17, 2020

Senator The Honourable Kamina Johnson Smith
Minister of Foreign Affairs and Foreign Trade
Ministry of Foreign Affairs and Foreign Trade
21 Dominica Drive
Kingston

Dear Senator Johnson,

RE: Referral of Petition to Her Majesty for Reparation for Enslavement

I attach hereto for your information correspondence with Minister Olivia Grange and Attorney General Marlene Malahoo Forte that clearly sets out the procedure proposed in respect of my member's motion dated January 27, 2015 seeking reparation as indicated.

I seek your blessings and your confirmation so that I can get the government's position in moving forward.

Regards,
Central Clarendon

L. Michael Henry, OJ, CD, MP
Member of Parliament

MIKE HENRY, OJ, CD, MP.
CENTRAL CLARENDON

HOUSES OF PARLIAMENT
GORDON HOUSE,
DUKE STREET,
KINGSTON, JAMAICA
TELEPHONE: (876)938-0005
CELLPHONE: (876) 286-0740
FAX: (876)759-8752
EMAIL: michaelhenrylmh@yahoo.com

December 17, 2020

The Honourable Olivia Grange, CD, MP
Minister of Culture, Gender, Entertainment and Sports
Ministry of Culture, Gender, Entertainment and Sports
4-6 Trafalgar Road
Kingston

Dear Minister Grange,

RE: Referral of Petition to Her Majesty for Reparation for Enslavement

I write further to my private member's motion in parliament dated January 27, 2015 seeking reparation from the British government for enslavement of our people in Jamaica and, to inform you that I intend to pursue this claim as a Member of Parliament who represents a substantial number of citizen of Clarendon, the parish where the first resistance to slavery was carried out in Jamaica at Suttons plantation.

I attach hereto a correspondence relative to this matter that was shared with your ministry on the understanding that you would be actively interested in pursuing this claim to satisfy the motion for parliament.

I seek your blessing and your confirmation so that I can get the government's support in moving forward.

Regards,
Central Clarendon

L. Michael Henry, OJ, CD, MP
Member of Parliament

Epilogue

It is not every day that one gets to the point of having overwhelming evidential basis for a stated position, including testimonial support from virtually the proverbial 'horse's mouth'.

From the direct words of Prince Charles, heir to the British throne, in Africa in November 2018, it has been accepted that the empire's central involvement in the transatlantic slave trade was an appalling atrocity that has left an "indelible stain" on the world.

In acknowledging the "profound injustice" of the legacy of the slave trade and slavery and declaring that this should never be forgotten, Prince Charles added that "The appalling atrocity of the slave trade and the unimaginable suffering it caused, left an indelible stain on the history of our world", and said that, "While Britain can be proud that it later led the way in the abolition of this shameful trade, we have a shared responsibility to ensure that the abject horror of slavery is never forgotten".

Now if the Prince, on Britain's behalf, cannot forget the horrors of the slave trade and slavery, how else but through a process of full acknowledgement and atonement and an agreed formula of seeking to right the wrong through a process of reparation to better position the descendants of African slaves in the Caribbean to gradually overcome the psychological blow of the gross experience, can the actual victims get past the stain and stigma?

How else can the historical advocacy for reparation be finally resolved without due recognition of the fact that only five short years ago, the British Treasury was still paying on the loan the

British Government undertook centuries ago to compensate the slave owners for the loss of their human chattel, yet to this day, evident in the Windrush debacle the biggest losers in the whole system of chattel slavery for over 200 years and the psychological impact thereafter - the slaves themselves and their descendants – have not had the benefit of even the consideration of the British Government?

And how does one reconcile the realities of reparation concessions by both British and American institutions that have conceded to having significantly benefited from the economic spin-offs of the British plantation system in the Caribbean and Americas, with direct agreements on stream for compensation therefrom, with virtual stonewalling from the British Government?

This all comes within the historical context of warnings and advisories to British colonial administrations in the Caribbean amid the early onset of the transatlantic slave trade from West Africa to the Caribbean and the Americas from none other than the British Government and Monarchy.

So if you warned against it as an evil and exploitive venture at the outset; you have now deemed it to have been exactly that when it existed; and some of your loyal subjects and associated parties have now acknowledged responsibility and led by example with agreed programmes of activities towards resolutions, how come the same is being so stubbornly resisted in respect of Britain itself, the primary conspirator and chief architect in the implementation and execution of the slave system in the Caribbean region centuries ago?

Quite frankly, it is now no longer a matter of reasoning and advocacy, but one of decency and reality, a reality that can no longer be ignored and kept out of the broad public discourse on the future relationship between the Caribbean region and Britain, the traditional motherland, which now stands proven of having grossly exploited its colonial off-springs, instead of seeking to nurture them.

As a society which has traditionally prided itself on its principles, Britain simply needs to now face the reality that reparation is inevitable for the descendants of its once slave population in the Caribbean, and there is no better time than now to simply do what is both just and right!

Nothing less will be good enough.

So much time has passed between the crimes and the pending consequences, and it is to Jamaica and the Caribbean's credit that so much patience has been exhibited.

But that vine is coming to an end and only an agreed formula for Reparation will suffice to offer any chance of maintaining the publicly cordial but inwardly badly strained relationship between Britain and its historical Caribbean colonies, especially Jamaica, and any real possibility of rebuilding that relationship to the level where it ought to be.

References

Works Cited
(Pages 81, 84, 86, 87, 89, 118, 119, 120)

Edmond Campbell. “Jamaican MP Calls for Reparations for Slavery.” *Friday Gleaner*. Kingston: The Gleaner Company Limited, 2007. 2-16. Online.

Daraine Luton. “Parliament Not Ready to Take Vote on Reparation - Hanna” *Thursday Gleaner*. Kingston: The Gleaner Company Limited, 2012. 4-19. Online.

“Mike Henry to Boycott Parliament Over Reparations” *Wednesday Gleaner*. Kingston: The Gleaner Company Limited, 2012. 5-09. Online.

Daraine Luton. “Even ‘On a Stretcher’, Henry Vows to Continue Reparations Fight.” *Wednesday Gleaner*. Kingston: The Jamaica Observer, 2014. 9-22. Online.

Balford Henry. “House to Resume Reparations Debate.” *Monday Observer*. Kingston: The Gleaner Company Limited, 2013. 1-30. Online.

“PJ’s focus on scoring own goal instead of the real goal.” *Sunday Gleaner*. Kingston: The Gleaner Company Limited, 2020. 5-17. Print.

“Mike Henry scores own goal against PJ Patterson.” *Sunday Observer*. Kingston: The Jamaica Observer, 2020. 5-24. Print.

“Magical dreams and uncertain destiny - A response.” *Sunday Observer*. Kingston: The Jamaica Observer, 2020. 5-24. Print.

“Racism and slavery like a horse and carriage?” *Sunday Observer*. Kingston: The Jamaica Observer, 2020. 7-05. Print.

CPSIA information can be obtained
at www.ICGtesting.com
Printed in the USA
JSHW041404190121
11042JS00005B/10